A Win-Win Future

Chinese Economy in the Age of Globalisation

U0095578

Huang Weiping Ding Kai Lai Mingming Liu Yijiao Song Yang Liu Kejia
Translated by Wang Shihua Huang Rikang

China Renmin University Press
Beijing

图书在版编目（CIP）数据

双赢的未来：全球化时代的中国经济：英文/黄卫平等著；王诗华，黄日康
译．—北京：中国人民大学出版社，2012.11
ISBN 978-7-300-16622-3

Ⅰ.①双…　Ⅱ.①黄…　②王…　③黄…　Ⅲ.①中国经济-经济发展-研究-英文
Ⅳ.①F124

中国版本图书馆 CIP 数据核字（2012）第 258371 号

双赢的未来：全球化时代的中国经济（英文版）

黄卫平　丁　凯　赖明明　刘一姣　宋　洋　刘可佳　著
王诗华　黄日康　译

出版发行	中国人民大学出版社			
社　　址	北京中关村大街 31 号		**邮政编码**	100080
电　　话	010－62511242（总编室）		010－62511398（质管部）	
	010－82501766（邮购部）		010－62514148（门市部）	
	010－62515195（发行公司）		010－62515275（盗版举报）	
网　　址	http://www.crup.com.cn			
	http://www.ttrnet.com（人大教研网）			
经　　销	新华书店			
印　　刷	涿州市星河印刷有限公司			
规　　格	155mm×230mm　16 开本		**版　　次**	2012 年 11 月第 1 版
印　　张	11　插页 1		**印　　次**	2012 年 11 月第 1 次印刷
字　　数	183 000		**定　　价**	138.00 元

目录
Contents

Introduction

Global trends are massive. Go with the trends, and you will prosper. Go against them, and you are doomed.

(1)

The foundation for any development is economic development. Any recovery starts with economic recovery.

In the present world, the Chinese economy, along with the Chinese factor behind it, is a research field with tremendous value. How does China join hands with other countries to drive the development of the global economy? How to cooperate and eliminate the factor of uncertainty in the global economy? This requires the direct coupling of the interests of the politicians, academics and experts, entrepreneurs and investors. And increasingly this is related to the direct interests of every world citizen.

Economic research is not just dry numbers and models. It is also a vibrant and colorful area of study indirectly related to life, leisure, consumption, and even sports. For instance, behind the Olympics and the World Cup is a competition of economic power among various nations.

Since the Vuvuzela was blown aloud in the 2011 World Cup in South Africa, every international sports event has had significant links with the term "Made in China". In the 2012 London Olympics, the Chinese language, Chinese words, Chinese restaurants and Chinese enterprises were seen everywhere. In fact, the "Made in China" sign has become the most prominent Chinese element in the London Olympics. According to statistics released by the International Olympics Committee, 65% of the franchised products sold at the London Olympics were made in China. In addition, the uniforms of the US delegation as well as the "weird" berets were manufactured by an enterprise in Dalian, China. Meanwhile, the ceremonial uniforms of the British Olympic delegation were produced by an enterprise in Yantai, China. And countries like Iran and Kazakhstan chose the sportswear produced by Chinese brands.

Since Mr. Liu Changchun represented China to take part in the 1932 Olympics, right up to the 2012 London Olympics, phenomenal changes have taken place in the Chinese sports arena, and this also reflects the cataclysmic changes in the Chinese economy over the past eight decades.

Indeed, the development of the Chinese economy has become a global trend in the present world. Economic development is not only changing China, it is also influencing the world. In today's globalised world, China and other countries are doing what they each are good at, and this has created a situation in the trading industry where "You are among us and we are among you". Originally this is the result of optimal allocation of resources, but it also created a controversy around "Made in China". This even became a good excuse for the rise of trade protectionism.

What we should pay even more attention to is that most of the consumers in the West have a totally opposite attitude to "Made in China" vis-à-vis people who hold an extreme view. In the eyes of ordinary consumers in the West, commodities are commodities, and there is no need to attach a political label to the same commodities. To them, "Made in China" equates to quality goods at low prices, which brings benefits to ordinary consumers.

Several years ago, a US business journalist Sara Bongiorni （邦吉奥尼） studied data from the US Ministry of Commerce （美国商务部） and found that the US imported large quantities of commodities from China every year. She then persuaded her family to try out living a life free from "Made in China" commodities for a year starting from 1 January 2005. During the year, Bongiorni found that her daily life had become much more inconvenient and even difficult. Since she would not buy Chinese products, she had to boil water to prepare coffee after her coffee kettle broke down. After her stirrer broke down, she could not repair it because the blade to be replaced was made in China. In order to identify non-Chinese-made commodities, she spent a lot of extra time and efforts, and also had to pay much higher prices.

After a year, she wrote a book called *A Year without "Made in China"* to share her experience and insights, and vowed never to do this again. While admitting that Chinese goods had occupied the major consumer goods market in the US, she stated in even clearer terms that "Made in China" benefited the ordinary US citizens the most, particularly the people in the low to medium income group.

From the micro perspective, "Made in China" means "Chinese products". From the macro perspective, it represents the Chinese economy. Whether you are willing to admit it or not, consumers all over the world—from the London Olympics to the ordinary US consumer—have endorsed "Made in China", "Chinese products" and even the Chinese economy by their choice and action.

(2)

It was the best of times; it was the worst of times. It was the season of light; it was the season of darkness. It was the spring of hope; it was the winter of despair. When we ponder Charles Dickens' famous lines, you and I will be astonished to find that after 200 years have passed, the current world is still at the crossroads of contradiction typified by Dickens. Indeed, the world's future depends very much on our choices today.

From the standpoint of reason, we can take a realistic look at "Made in China", "Chinese products" and the Chinese economy. We can even look at the renaissance of China, which has gone beyond China itself to become a global issue.

In the past century, it was extremely difficult for a developing country to become a great global economy. After a century of vicissitude and 30 years of superb management and positive effort, China has risen to the global economic stage to play a key role. While we can summarise the modes of development of the Chinese economy from different perspectives, we must stress a few things.

First, China abandoned a confined and secluded nation, and insisted on opening itself to the world, and actively linking with the global economy. As a result, there is a beneficial interaction between the Chinese economy and the economies of the rest of the world.

Second, China abandoned its planned economy in favor of market economy. In the operation of the socialist market economy, China fully demonstrated the advantage of its unique, highly efficient and unified policy formulation and implementation.

Third, good policies and systems have enabled the Chinese people to make good use of their racial characteristics of diligence, bravery and endurance. When China's advantage in human resources is put to good use, the inexhaustible workforce will become the engine of wealth generation, bringing benefits to consumers around the world.

China has exhibited its strength and perseverance in its systems, policies and operations. When this is in line with the global trends, the development of the Chinese economy is the inevitable outcome. The importance of the Chinese economy to China is evident. The next question is—what is the importance of China's economic growth to the world? Is the Chinese economy "good" or "bad" for China itself and the world at large?

The key to evaluating the Chinese economy is to determine the criteria. We propose the following two criteria—one is the humanistic criterion. For any economic growth, if it is not of benefit to the development of the people, this kind of economic development cannot be labeled as "good". The development of human society boils down to the development of the people. This is globally true. The other criterion is based on the common interest across the globe. If any economic development is beneficial only to its own country and not to other countries or regions, this economic development is not a "good" one. In other words, economic growth needs to be win-win and mutually beneficial.

Ⅰ. About the first criterion—the relationship between the development of the Chinese economy and the development of "people". One approach to economic research is to start from the production factors. Production factors refer to various social resources needed for social production and operation. In general, they include land, natural resources, manpower, capital, science and technology, intellectual property, information, and the quality of the entrepreneur. Be it Western classical economics represented by Adam Smith and David Ricardo, or the doctrines of Karl Marx's labor theory of value, the emphasis is always the value of the workforce and its contribution to economic growth.

In 2011, China's average per capita GDP was RMB 35,198.57 (or US$5,414), and the per capita disposable income in cities and towns was RMB 23,979. Although this is not ranked high in the global chart, yet the growth rate and duration are both ranked among the world top economies when compared against 1979 at the start of China's reform and open policy, when the per capita GDP was only RMB 416, and the disposable income in the cities and towns was only RMB 387.

China's economic growth not only testifies to the vitality of the theory of labor value in classical economics, it also testifies to the recognition of the capabilities of entrepreneurs in the book *Principles of Economics* by Marshall. Whether it is general labor, or the capabilities of entrepreneurs, it can be grouped under the "human" factor. The major endowment of China's economy is not in natural resources, but on "people". The "human" factor has played a decisive role in China's economic development, and this is where the power of "people" becomes evident.

II. About the second criterion—the relationship between China's economic development and the world's economic development. Looking at China's economy from the standpoint of global interest, the development in the past three odd decades, especially in the decade or so after China's accession to WTO, we can say that instead of the China factor impacting on the global economy, the truth is that the Chinese economy and the global economy have formed a mutually complementary beneficial cycle where both share their triumphs and defeats. China's economic development has never aimed to achieve it's own dominance. Rather, the goal has always been to achieve mutual prosperity as it pursues its own development.

French classical economist Quesnay in his book *Tableau Economique* puts emphasis on economic cycles and their similarity to the blood circulation system of the human body. If a beneficial cycle is maintained between production and consumption, among various production units and various countries, then the economy can maintain steady growth. On the other hand, all economic crises are the result of the failure to maintain a normal economic cycle. China's economic growth has always insisted on integration and interaction with the global economy. Today, the Chinese economy has become a part of the global economy, and both have formed a cycle. Based on this close and mutually beneficial relationship, the sustainability of the Chinese economic model comes as no surprise.

Whether from the human perspective or based on global interest, any inspection of the Chinese economy will yield this conclusion: the Chinese economy has created a good era for the country itself, and has also created a good start for the global economy.

China's economic growth has transformed the world in the following aspects:

First, China's commodities have not only brought benefits to consumers all over the world, but also they have eliminated the "stagnation" that has plagued the economic growth in Western countries for many years. China's exports have reduced the inflation rate in different parts of the world (especially in the US), benefiting the ordinary consumers. To the ordinary people in the US, clothing, daily necessities and electronic products that are "Made in China" have become part of life for the majority of Americans. According to data from the Chinese Embassy in the US, Chinese commodities in the past decade have saved over US＄600 billion for the US consumers, increasing the disposable income for an average US family by US＄1,000.

Second, the development of China's manufacturing industry has filled the gap left by insufficient capacity in the US manufacturing industry, building a robust platform for the restructuring of the US economy, and indirectly promoting the development of high technology and venture investments in the US new industry by eliminating the worries in the process. China's manufacturing industry, which is huge, highly efficient and comprehensive, has not only created a haven for global financial capital, it has brought massive profits for foreign capital financial companies entering the Chinese market. Statistics show that in the past nearly 10 years, China has used over US$1,000 billion.

Moreover, the scale and dynamics of the Chinese market not only affect the global strategies of multinational companies, but they also promote the development of these companies. Hence the Chinese market has become an important part of the global production chain. Indeed, China is an irreplaceable link in the global production chain and even the global purchasing chain. A large number of multinational corporations will set up their supply chain as an indispensable part of their global strategy. Today, any multinational corporation that needs to complete the chain of design, purchasing, production and sales cannot do so without having a presence in China.

Finally, the needs of China not only affect the price trends of international commodities, but they also stabilise the growth of the global economy. Take the iron and steel industry as an example. 10 years ago China imported 92. 3 million tons of iron ore. Then the figure increased to 400 million in 2008, and 600 million in 2011, making the country the world's largest importer of iron ore. This enables countries with rich natural resources, like Australia, Brazil, Canada, Middle East countries and Southeast Asian countries, to have a steady flow of foreign currency income.

(3)

The development of the Chinese economy is a historical process. Since 1949 there have been two distinct stages in China's economic development. 1978 marked the start of "the Chow's Test" as propounded by famous Chinese origin American economist Prof Gregory Chow. Prior to this, China was a relatively closed economy, and economic development was relatively slow. Then China opened itself up, and its economy enjoyed a sustainable growth, and its strength continued to increase, resulting in a steady rise in the people's standard of living. In the meantime, China's status in the global economy has been on the rise, with an increasing impact on the international scene.

Indeed, December 1978 was the turning point in the Chinese economy. The 3rd plenary session of the 11th Central Committee of the Communist Party determined the national policy of reform and opening-up. Then in 1979, Deng Xiaoping visited Washington DC in the US, and made a historical handshake between China and the US. Lee Kuan Yew, then Prime Minister of Singapore, said after hearing this, "China will never close its door again!"

In 1999, about 10 years later, Chinese President Jiang Zemin had a telephone meeting with then US President Bill Clinton. This heralded in the resumption of talks on China's entry into the World Trade Organization (WTO). Two years later, China officially became a member of the WTO. A year or so later, US representative in the WTO talks, Charlene Barshefsky, said in a seminar, "The rise of the Chinese economy has been the greatest change in the global trade and investment arena. In fact, this is the greatest change on the international trade and commerce scene in over a century. China is changing the face of Asia, promoting growth in the global economy, and possibly changing the status of political influences at the international level."

About a decade later, in 2008, another momentous event took place—also in Washington. Chinese President Hu Jintao attended "the Group of 20 (G-20) Summit", and held discussions with political leaders all over the world on reforming the global financial system. Shortly before this summit, former French President Jacques Chirac stressed, "Without China's participation, we cannot possibly hold any meaningful discussion on global issues like the financial crisis, climate change, and energy resources."

The establishment of the new China, especially its economic development in the over three decades after the period of reform and opening-up, shows that China is not just passively accepting the influences of the external world, but also actively learning from the achievements of humankind in terms of advanced productivity and advanced civilization. At the same time, China has made tremendous contributions to world prosperity and stability.

In today's world, no country can afford to neglect the rise of China. No multinational corporation is willing to give up the Chinese market, and no economics scholar can turn a blind eye on China's influence. Global affairs call on China's participation. Global patterns need China's rise. Global balance requires China's power.

On the one hand, China has made economic achievements that the West world finds hard to comprehend. On the other hand, China has provided a success story on economic development for reference by other countries.

When we cast our sight on how China integrated itself in the development trends of world economies, and seriously appreciate the vicissitudes over the past three odd decades, we are bound to draw a common conclusion that the fate of China and the world are more and more integrated. China's interests are the world's interests; the world's interests are China's interests. In interacting with the world, China has been growing its own economy, and this has made a profound impact on the world's political and economic scene, and has provided new opportunities for the development of other countries.

A great era has begun. This is the era of mutually beneficial interactions between China and the world.

(4)

In the three decades or so since China started to implement its reform and opening-up policy, the country has basically established a vibrant socialist market economy system. China has consistently maintained an economic growth rate that is higher than the global average; its GDP and per capita GDP has dramatically risen, and its status in the global economy has fundamentally changed. Indeed, China has become one of the engines for the world economic growth.

The renaissance of China is the focus of global attention, and a challenging topic for academic research. It is also an issue that has strong political undertones.

Due to various reasons, the international community has long been ignorant of how the Chinese economy is developing and its direction and modes. Different people have grasped certain characteristics, such as the "cheap labour theory", "foreign capital motivation theory", "export pulling theory", and "authoritative government theory". However, these represent only part of the picture, but fail to provide a holistic and accurate explanation of China's economic development.

While the world enjoys the benefits brought by the sustained development of the Chinese economy, and delights in this progress, some foreign media have been invalidating the development mode of the Chinese economy, or limiting this mode to China's specific historical setting, thereby generating the theories of "China's collapse" and "China's threat".

These voices have accompanied China's economic development process over the past 30 odd years, and have made themselves heard in the international community. The Chinese who have experienced the reform and opening-up of China will understand this—the world needs time to understand and accept China's economic development model. Indeed, China in its development process will inevitably encounter a diversity of problems and issues, and both applause and criticism will accompany the process all the way. All of these are a test for the Chinese people's determination in holding onto their characteristic mode of development, and also an exercise in their patience in winning the world's understanding. We do not pursue universal understanding of China's renaissance, yet we firmly believe that China will definitely win more and more understanding and trust. More and more friends will join hands with China to achieve world peace and human prosperity.

In fact, China's economic development has never been marred by the "China collapse theory" or the "China threat theory". Rather, it has subtle harmony, motivation and self-encouragement, insisting on the key motif of "development being the hard truth".

The three decades of China's reform and opening-up has proven that China will not collapse, and it will not constitute a threat. China's renaissance is a developing process along the main theme of China's sustained economic development. This is the trend of the world, and the logic of history. This process not only takes the form of GDP growth, but it also accompanies the renaissance of the Chinese culture with the values of loyal, piety, benevolence, love, trust and virtue as the core. This results in the strengthening of the power that maintains world peace.

The three decade's sustained economic growth in China also proves that there are no deities in the world, and economic development does not depend on any saviour. It also shows that there is no single economic development model for the entire world, or there is not a path of economic development that is absolutely correct. What is reasonable will continue to exist, and what exists is reasonable. A scientific road of development is one that is based on fact, one that starts with the national reality, and one that is people-oriented. China's economic achievements are the result of the determination to go down the path adapted to conditions in China, and to insist on a people-oriented scientific outlook on development.

While history will not repeat itself, it encompasses startling similarities. 500 years ago the western part of the Asian-European continent welcomed the light of the Renaissance. Today, the eastern part of the Asian-European continent is going through another great renaissance. "Go your own way regardless of what people say " —this is the track record of the European Renaissance, and a reflection of China's economic development.

(5)

China's renaissance is the result of abandonment, opening-up, and consolidation. China's development is based on the best of the Chinese traditional philosophy and culture, as well as the world's advanced productivity and cultural wisdom. China has creatively carved out its development path and mode that ride on world trends and are in harmony with the national realities.

China's renaissance is holistic, with economic development as the key melody. A comprehensive summary of China's economic growth, accurately deciphering China's economic development, effectively elimi-nates the misconceptions about China's economic development—these are not only conducive to enabling China to achieve an even more robust development process, but also help developing countries to map out their own development path that suits their own national realities. Mo-reover, this also enriches and deepens the study of development eco-nomics.

Some people think that after a country has developed its economy, a sort of parochial nationalism will emerge, suggesting expansionism and hegemony. However, this is not a universal pattern, and this senti-mental attitude needs to be questioned.

Historically China has attached great importance to "courtesy" and "virtuousness", and the country has been hailed as a country of courtesy and modesty. On the Silk Road, what China exported was silk, ceramics and culture, and not expansionism. When Zheng He sailed to the western seas, what he brought from China was advanced agricultur-al and textile technologies, and not invasion. The Chinese element is in essence the element of peace.

Based on a respect for history and an observation of the reality, we can conclude that the sustained development of the Chinese economy is an increase in the power of peace in the world. Indeed, the power of China is the power of peace.

In recent years, China can say "no", and this has become a common saying. Firstly, we must make it clear that China is not saying "no" for the sake of saying "no". Secondly, the ability of China to say "no" is not the consequence of the increase in China's economic strength, and China's economic development is not the result of China's ability to say "no". Since the setting up of the new China, China has dared to say "no" even in the face of widespread depression and limited economic strength. In the face of hegemony and authoritarianism, China has dared to say "no".

Hence, China dares to say "no" in the face of elements not condu-cive to world and regional peace, and elements not conducive to promo-ting world and regional prosperity.

The process of China's sustainable economic development is the process of increasing world peace and prosperity. On the one hand, we urge the world to look at China's sustainable development and renaissance in a positive light. On the other hand, we will look at the development of other countries from a wider perspective and with a more open-minded attitude. With more patience, we look forward to more and more friends understanding and accepting China's rise to become an economic power.

(6)

While the international economy and the natural environment are fundamentally different, yet both require balance. Balance, discipline and moderation are the safeguard for the normal operation of any system.

Balance is maintaining harmony in nature, and the gravitational force that maintains the running of the heavenly bodies. Balance is also the basis for the normal operation of economies. The loss of balance is the loss of cycles, and without cycles, there is no circulation and exchange, and this affects production and consumption. Of course, balance is dynamic balance, rather than static balance where nothing changes. Balance can be interrupted temporarily, but a long-term loss of balance will bring economic operations to a halt.

The economic system today is a pyramid with the US occupying the top echelon, and with developed countries like Japan and European countries on the next. At the bottom of the pyramid are the developing countries and new market economies.

In nature, the lion king that occupies the top of the food chain lives on animals that feed on plants. However, it will not over-greedily kill all the plant-eating animals—of course it does not have such an appetite. The balance between carnivores and herbivores, and that between herbivores and plants, maintain the cycle of regeneration in nature.

However, the greed and ambition of Wall Street go far beyond the greed and ambition of the lion king. In essence, Wall Street is a synonym for international capital dominated by the US, and international capital is the capitalization of human greed. Old colonialism used weapons to carry out invasion in oceans. New colonialism uses currency and modern financial tricks to make a profit in the capital market.

To be able to flex its muscles, international capital requires loose foreign exchange control, a financial system that enables a free flow of capital and global alignment. Finally this opportunity comes.

In 1997, international capital took advantage of the weakness of newly industrialised Asian countries that had been expanding too fast without the support of sufficient foreign currency reserve to wage a financial war. As a result, it robbed Asia's four dragons and another five tigers of their wealth accumulated for several decades. At the critical moment during the regional economic crisis, China extended a helping hand by insisting that the Renminbi, Chinese currency will not depreciate. The country bought large amounts of commodities from Korea and Southeast Asia, to help these countries weather the economic crisis to regain their economic balance and resume their economic growth.

About a decade later—in 2008—international capital changed its strategy and created a financial tsunami on an even larger scale than before. They craftily converted their own property loan crisis into a global crisis, pushing the financial tsunami to the Asian-European region, causing the virtual economy to impact on the real economy. Again, at the critical moment of this global economic crisis, China took important action to stabilise the global economy.

At the turn of the century, the balance in the global economy was twice broken each time by a serious financial crisis. This exposed the greed of Wall Street, and testified to China's active contribution to stabilising the global economy.

Wall Street's greed is inborn. In the process of disrupting the balance in the world economy, it reaps an exorbitant profit. The hope that Wall Street will give up its greed will be futile. Rather than hoping a carnivore to change into a herbivore, it would be better to promote the establishment of a new order in the international economic arena, and to call on the power of China in maintaining a balanced scene in the world economy.

Should we maintain or reform the international economic scene?

The world trend is to invalidate the Wall Street international capital as an agent of change. We forecast that it will be unrealistic to expect international financial crises to disappear. However, the power of China will help smooth out the waves of the world economic crisis. The change of the international economic system from the pyramid structure to a balanced structure will be hard to realize even with advocacy, but the China factor will be an active force in facilitating developing countries to pursue world economic balance.

(7)

Since Adam Smith advocated international division of labour and international trade, economists have all been pursuing the effective allocation of resources, economic sustainability, and the sustainable increase in human welfare.

When the news bulletin is filled with stories about financial crises, stock market collapses, exchange rate fluctuations, debt crises, widening gaps between the rich and poor, deterioration of the ecology, and regional strife, all world citizens—not just economists—are contemplating the same issues: How to narrow the gap between the rich and the poor? How to maintain a balanced growth in the global economy? And how to sustainably enhance the common welfare of mankind?

Today's global issues point to the critical need for a change in the current international economic system, and the establishment of a new order in the global economy.

For an extended period, the world economy will be characterised by sluggish growth, structural adjustment, coopetition and consolidation in commerce and trade, and confrontation and conflict. It will be the hope of the people that the China factor will become the factor for the growth and stability of the global economy, that China's economic growth and China's renaissance will be the key to the establishment of a new order in the international economy, that the China power will be key to a new balance in the international economic system, and that a mode of sharing in the economic growth will become the best option for resolving the conflicts in today's global economy.

Internally, the benefit sharing mode is evident in the coordinated growth of countries and the welfare of their people. The national economic policy can, on the basis of strengthening social productivity (or on the basis of the enhancement and transformation of the economic development mode), progressively establish a system for the sharing of social wealth, thereby improve the people's quality of life.

Externally, the benefit sharing mode is evident in the shared growth between developed countries and developing countries. The economic development mode that allows only rich countries to have their way and neglects the welfare of poor countries has no market in the global arena. Even if there is such a market, it will be transitory and never permanent.

The aim of this book is to enable local and overseas readers to appreciate the features of China's economic development and its role in the global economy of tomorrow, and to share our aspirations for the future growth of the world economy. However, this is clearly not where the fun of writing is. The fun of writing is in the process of data collection, research, analysis and deduction. To enjoy the fun of writing, one must give up any existing conclusions, letting the data speak, and letting the facts draw their own conclusions.

As we put pen to paper, we were surprised to find that all the facts and figures point to one thing—China's renaissance is the world trend; the power of China is the power to achieve economic balance, and the sharing mode of growth is the global trend of thought. So our ultimate goal is actually to synchronise with the enjoyment of the process!

German evangelist Albert Schweitzer has this assessment of humanity: The optimist only looks at the green light, the pessimist only looks at the red light, and the real wise man is colour-blind. On this assumption, the promoters, navigators, participants, shouters, thinkers, doubters and critics of China's economy over the past three decades are all wise men.

Finally, let us look forward to a better future—for the world and for the Chinese economy!

Part 1

Facts and Figures

The Global Economy "Dancing with the Dragon"

From "Layman" to "Master": China's Accession to WTO Tilts the Balance of the Global Economy

Since its reform and opening-up, China has chosen to develop its own way of economic development. It follows rather than challenging the game rules of the global economy, and actively takes part in, rather than isolating itself from, the global economy.

On 11 July 1986, China officially requested to resume its membership of the General Agreement on Tariffs and Trade (GATT). From that point onward, the new China had been on the GATT-resumption path for over eight years. From 1 January 1995, with the establishment of the World Trade Organisation (WTO), China spent nearly seven years on its bid to access to the WTO.

The critical moment came at 7:30 pm Doha (capital of Qatar) time on 11 November 2001, or 12:30 am Beijing time on 12 November, at the Al Majlis Conference Hall at Doha Sheraton Hotel. The then China's Minister of Foreign Economic Relations and Trade, Mr Shi Guangsheng, represented China's Government, signed the official document prepared by director of Legal Affairs Division of WTO . After 30 days, China officially became the 143rd member of the WTO.

The then WTO Director-General, Mr Mike Moore, said at the signing ceremony, "We need China to play a leading role in economic development. The global economy is slackening, and a lot of employment opportunities will be lost. Hence China's accession to the WTO is not only a historic moment for China, but also for WTO and the world. " If this exciting moment represents the end of a lengthy series of talks that is full of twists and turns, then it also suggests that China is starting to march towards the economic globalisation with a broader vision and a stronger determination, and at an even faster pace.

According to WTO's requirements of the principle of transparency, China implemented broad-brushed reforms with an iron fist, in a bid to enhance the transparency of the legislative process. From the central government laws, to the over 3,000 regulations of the 30 government departments, and to the 190,000 rules and systems of local authorities, everything was cleared or adjusted. The reversal system formed by external pressure has expedited the changes in the functions of the Chinese Government. Looking back on the development path of the Chinese economy, we will find that the difficulties and efficiency of these measures were hard to be easily assessed through numbers.

China's accession to the WTO means it has changed from a mere spectator to a player. Playing the game of global trade is like we assume a double role of both the player and the umpire, changing our face every now and then. The player who participates more in the game rules will be the one who enjoys more of the benefits of global trade. China's metamorphosis from a cabby to an international star is progressive, starting from zero.

Less than a month after China's accession to the WTO, the 4th Ministerial Conference of WTO was held in Doha. China took part in the meeting in the capacity of an observer because it needed one month to confirm China's membership. When developed countries such as the US and the European Union confronted developing countries headed by India, Mr Shi Guangsheng chose to do shopping. At that time, China's

Vice Minister of the Ministry of Foreign Trade and Economic Cooperation and chief WTO negotiator Mr Long Yongtu was relaxing in the swimming pool. Mr Long's feeling at that time was, "During the WTO talks, the situation was—the minority was negotiating, while the majority was drinking coffee. "

In 2005, WTO's 6th Ministerial Conference was held in Hong Kong. China took part in all the seven "Green Room Meetings" with only 32 participants. (The official name of Green Room is CCG, or Chairmen's Consultative Group—the most important talk venue in WTO.) China expressed its views on major issues, becoming a member that drinks coffee on the one hand, and a "minority person" in the talks on the other hand.

For instance, paragraph 6 of the Hong Kong Manifesto states that all the members should cancel their agricultural export subsidies by 2013. The 110 member countries of six organisations, such as ACP Group formed by the island countries in the Carribean Sea and the Pacific Ocean, signed a joint declaration that demands the abandonment of all subsidies in 2010. However, the European Union insisted that this deadline should be extended to 2013. This issue then became the tug-of-war focus in the Green House Talks. As various parties held on to their positions, China suggested that on the basis of rigorous and clear conditions, the plan propounded by the European Union to cancel export subsidy in 2013 should be accepted. This was endorsed by India's and Mexico's Green House members.

Once the outsider enters the house, he becomes one of the masters in the house. In today's global market, no one can afford to neglect China's voice. As "Made in China" runs towards the global market, as an unprecedentedly large and new market, China becomes one of the greatest countries that absorbs the largest amount of foreign direct investment. As at the end of 2010, over 90% of the 500 largest enterprises have started businesses in China, and there are over 1,400 companies set up by multinational corporations in China.

The gigantic China market not only affects the price fluctuations of international commodities, it also has bearing on the global strategies of multinational corporations. At present, all the corporations in the world are interested in the tastes of Chinese consumers—they set up their R&D centres in China, put their core purchasing function in China, and without doubt, the China market is the centre of attention for many financial statements of multinational corporations. At the same time, the progressively robust Chinese enterprises are setting off to compete in the global market.

Of course, in the arena of world trade, China, as an outstanding athlete, has often been questioned by cynics as a player of dubious integrity. In the decade following China's accession to WTO, China answered and clarified over 3,500 queries raised by WTO members, making it the "most diligent" candidate in any test imaginable in the world. Putting all the answers together, the number of words amounted to 500 million, which is equivalent to 2 million copies of *Steve Jobs: A Biography*, or 3 million copies of the *Bible*.

When China entered into WTO, the Chinese were worried about "dancing with the wolf". After its accession, China transformed itself and impacted the world at an astounding speed and with tremendous passion. Today, in the face of the consolidated strengths of Chinese enterprises, the hot topic in international discussions is how to "dance with the dragon".

China's accession to WTO has accelerated the world's embrace of China and the process of China's integration with the world. This has had positive and profound influences on China's economy and the global economy. China's development brings opportunities to the world, and the soaring of the great dragon benefits both China and the world. China's peaceful development has not constituted, and will not constitute, any threat to the world. On the opposite, it will definitely bring more opportunities and benefits. Indeed, armed with a workforce of high quality and low pay, as well as a huge economic scale coupled with high technology, China has become one of the greatest beneficiaries in economic globalisation.

From "B+" to "A+": A Diligent Student in the Testing Ground on Global Economy

When we look back on the decade following China's accession to

WTO, we will remember that in the early years, people in different fields were worried that the move would impact China's national economy, the employment market, and even agriculture, foreign trade, financial market, cars etc. The outcome was that the world did not shake China. On the other hand, China stunned the world. China's economy has acquired unprecedented space for development, with rapid growing strength. In the words of Mr Pascal Lamy, WTO Director-General, China's performance in the first decade of its accession to WTO was A+.

From 2001 to 2010, China's Gross Domestic Product (GDP) grew sustainably at 10.5% a year—from US $1,300 billion in 2001 to US $7,500 billion in 2011—an increase of over 5 times. In 2002, China's GDP overtook Italy and became the world's 6th largest economy. From 2005 to 2007, China got three promotions, with its GDP overtaking France, UK and Germany, to gain a place in the world's three greatest economies. In 2010, China with its economic growth of 10.4% and a total GDP of RMB 40,150 billion (equivalent to about US $6,000 billion), became the world's second biggest economy, outperforming Japan, who had occupied this position for over 40 years.

In the 10 years, after accession to WTO, China's dependency on foreign trade grew from under 40% prior to WTO entry to 50%, progressively expanding its market access in agriculture and manufacturing. Meanwhile, the total tariff level dropped from 15.3% to 9.8%. China also abandoned all its non-tariff measures such as the quota system and permits, and completely opened up its foreign trade operating rights for outside parties. For instance, the tariff for agricultural products in 2005 decreased from 23.2% before China's accession to WTO to 15.35%, much lower than that of developed countries like the US, Japan, and the European Union. In fact China is now one of the countries with the lowest tariffs for agricultural products. Due to the cutting of tariffs and export subsidies, China's growth in agricultural imports far exceeded its growth in agricultural exports. A trade deficit first appeared in 2004, and this deficit is set to increase year by year, and China became the largest importer of the agricultural product in the world.

In 2001, China's exports in commodities trading amounted to US $509.7 billion. This grew to US $1,100 billion in 2004, three years after WTO entry—a twofold increase. That year, China's export growth rate set a new record of 35.4%. In 2010, exports increased to US $2,970 billion—a 20.2% average annual growth within 10 years, and a total growth of 4.8 times. Meanwhile, the total trade soared to world No. 2 from No. 6. In this decade, the size of exports increased 4.9 times to gain top place in the world, accounting for 10.4% of the world total. Meanwhile, import size grew 4.7 times, occupying second place in the world, accounting for 9.1% of the global import figure, as compared with 3.8% prior to WTO entry.

In the 10 years in WTO, China optimised its foreign trade structure both in quantity and quality. From the standpoint of export commodities, manufactured products accounted for only 90.1% of the total commodities exports in 2001. The figure increased to 94.8% in 2007, and maintained at this high level in the ensuing four years. Correspondingly, primary products such as agriculture and mining products as well as raw materials accounted for 10% of the commodities exports in 2001, but dropped to 5.2% in 2010. In recent years, the Chinese Government promoted the transformation of the structure and mode of foreign trade growth, and products that suffer from high energy consumption and high emissions were under effective control, and high-tech products and products with high value-added became the new focus of growth.

From the standpoint of trade method, China's foreign trade demonstrated the formation of "balance + surplus + deficit". Trade in general goods is basically balanced, but there is a trade surplus in processing goods, and a deficit in service trading.

In the decade following China's accession to WTO, China's total service trading increased fourfold from US $71.9 billion to US $362.4 billion. The total service trading imports and exports ranked No. 9 and 12 respectively in 2001, and they rose to No. 3 and No. 4 respectively in 2010. China is progressively expanding its market access for the service industry. Among the 160 plus service trading departments based on WTO's categorisation, as many as 100 are already opened up, which is close to the level of developed countries.

As the saying goes, "If you have planted phoenix trees, then you don't have to worry about the phoenixes not coming. " In the eyes of foreign businessmen, China's opening-up policy has become more stable and more transparent. In the decade in which China was in WTO, China has attracted a cumulative US $ 759. 5 billion from foreign businessmen, with an average annual growth of 10%, maintaining its top position within developing countries in the last 20 years. Even in 2009 when the impact of the international financial crisis was the most serious, foreign investments still exceeded US $ 90 billion. In 2010, China actually used US $ 105. 74 billion in foreign capital, exceeding US $ 100 billion for the first time. It reversed the falling trend in the decrease of 2. 6% in 2009. On the other hand, there was an increase of 17. 4% compared with the same period in the previous year, accounting for 9. 4% of the world total, and ranking second globally.

Direct investments cannot be single-directional—only in and no out. In 2002, the Chinese Government proposed the "going out" strategy on top of the "coming in" strategy. Over the decade, the Government built its own structure on a pilot basis, and gradually started to boldly introduce equity investment as well as merger and acquisition. Chinese entrepreneurs explored their own path by diligently learning and reflecting, and through trial and error. This is still continuing. In 2012, China's Geely Automobile acquired Sweden's Volvo, and this was reported in both Chinese and European publications. At that time, neither the Auto industry nor the labour unions were optimistic about the future of this move. However, after several years of development, building an international team and accumulating highly market-driven local operations, and practising price negotiations, Chinese enterprises grew rapidly to become an integral part of the global market.

For various industries in China, direct foreign investment is starting to show positive elementary results. Some provinces grew rapidly, with annual growth rates ranging from 40% to 80%, even faster than the growth rate in the foreign capital capture phase. In 2002, China's non-financial enterprises registered direct foreign investments of only

US＄2.7 billion, but in 2005 the figure soared to over US＄10 billion. In 2010, China's all-industry direct foreign investments ranked No. 5 in the world, with a total investment of US＄68.81 billion, an increase of 24 times over 2002. Non-financial investments accounted for 87.5％, amounting to US＄60.18 billion, an increase of 25.9％ (See Table 1.1 and Figure 1.1). Chinese enterprises have been discharging their social responsibilities in their host country. As at 2010, they have employed nearly 800,000 local staff, and paid local taxes of over US＄10 billion annually.

Table 1.1   In the past decade China witnessed a steady increase in direct external investment in terms of stock and flow (US＄100 million)

year	2002	2003	2004	2005	2006	2007	2008	2009	2010
Flow	27.0	28.5	55.0	122.6	211.6	265.1	559.1	565.3	688.1
Stock	299.0	332.0	448.0	572.0	906.3	1,179.1	1,839.7	2,457.5	3,172.1

Note: 2002—2005 data refer to non-financial direct foreign investment; 2006—2010 figures refer to the direct investment figures for the entire profession.

Source: China's Ministry of Commerce, "Statistics on China's Direct Foreign Investments".

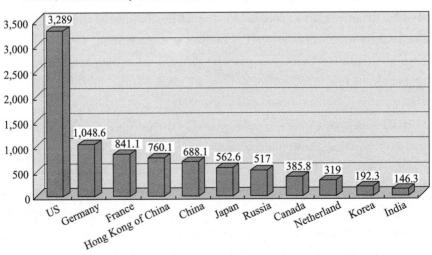

Figure 1.1   Compared with economies of Europe and the US, China's direct foreign investments have been dwarfed (US＄100 million)

Source: "2010 China Direct Foreign Investments Statistics" by China's Ministry of Commerce.

The decade following China's accession to WTO was the period in which China developed most rapidly and achieved the most. In 2001 China's average per capita income was US $ 800, and this increased to US $ 2,500 in 2009, and during that period, over 200 million Chinese people were freed from poverty. Based on the categorisation of the World Bank in 2011, China's label before the mid-1980s— "low income country" —has gone through "lower middle income country" to reach the status of "upper middle income country".

In that decade, China's foreign exchange reserves increased nearly 13 times, and in 1996, it was the first time it exceeded US $ 100 billion, in 2006 it exceeded the US $ 1,000 billion mark for the first time to reach US $ 1,066. 3 billion. In 2009, it exceeded the US $ 2,000 billion mark for the first time to reach US $ 2,399. 2 billion, and at the end of 2010, it reached US $ 2,850 billion. Under the influence of changes in the economic environment both inside and outside the country, the foreign exchange reserves have still been increasing, but at a slightly lower rate.

On 21 July 2005, after 11 years of RMB merging of exchange rate reforms, the People's Bank of China officially announced a managed floating foreign exchange rate policy, based on market demand and supply, and with reference to a basket of currencies. On that day, RMB's exchange rate against the US Dollar increased by 2. 01% from 8. 2765 to 8. 1100. Henceforth, the RMB exchange rate was no longer pegged to only the US Dollar. Thereafter, China has created a more flexible exchange rate mechanism. On 5 December that year, the five cities of Harbin and Changchun (both in the northeast of China), and Lanzhou, Yinchuan and Nanning (all in the west of China) started to enjoy RMB businesses operated by foreign capital organisations. This was one year ahead of the date promised by China as it entered into the WTO. At the same time, the China Banking Regulatory Commission also promised to open up this RMB business to Shantou and Ningbo. Thereafter, Chinese cities opened to foreign capital institutions increased from 18 to 25.

Being proactive, progressive and manageable has always characterised the RMB exchange rate reform in China. In July 2009, the pilot scheme for RMB clearing for cross border trade was officially commissioned. In June 2010, the clearing pilot sites expanded to 20 provinces, districts and cities, and overseas clearing sites were extended to all countries and regions. To effectively deal with the impacts of the 2008 international financial crisis, and to prevent the intrusion of "bad elements" from outside, the RMB exchange rate, for a certain period, was pegged to the US Dollar, and was maintained at the level of about 6. 82 for nearly a year. On 19 June 2010, China resumed the reform on RMB system. On 21 September 2010, 13 January, 29 April, and 11 August 2011, and on 10 February 2012, the medial rate in the US Dollar to RMB exchange rate broke through the 6. 7, 6. 6, 6. 5, 6. 4 and 6. 3 respectively.

From "Threat" to "Opportunities": Changes in China during the Global Financial Crisis

Since 2011, the profound impacts of the international financial crisis have continued, making it difficult for developed economies to revive. Since the last quarter, the debt crisis in the European countries have been fermenting and expanding, and the US economy in the first quater of 2012 has still been fragile. The Japanese economy is still fatigued, and the GDP growth rate in the second quarter significantly slackened. The economic growth rate for newly industrialized economies also slackened and was entangled with the inflation in commodity prices. In short, the global economy started to slacken, and the external needs for China were weak.

In the face of complex and threatening environments inside and outside the country, the Chinese economy maintained steady and rapid development, to give a good start to the 12th Five-year Plan period (2011 to 2015). According to the initial audits of the National Bureau of Statistics of China, while containing the commodity prices to an overall level of 5. 4%, the annual GDP in 2011 was RMB 47,156. 4 billion, an increase of 9. 2% over the previous year. In the first and second quarters of 2012, China's GDP reached RMB 22,709. 82 billion, an increase of 7. 8% over the same period in 2011 (See Figure 1. 2).

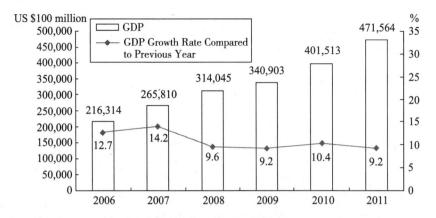

**Figure 1. 2　From 11th Five-year Plan to 12th Five-year Plan, the Chinese
economy weathered the adversities**

Source: National Bureau of Statistics of China, "2011 National Economic and Social Development Statistics".

On the foreign trade front, according to the statistics released by China Customs in January 2012, China's commodities import and export totalled US＄3,640 billion, an increase of 22. 5% over the corresponding period in the previous year. Export reached US＄1,900 billion, an increase of 20. 3%, and import was US＄1,740 billion, an increase of 24. 9%, and 4. 6% higher than the increase in export growth rate (See Figure 1. 3). Since the latter half of 2011, China's import and export trade growth rate slackened but the development of trade balanced—import and export developed in good coordination, and the surplus in foreign trade narrowed. The annual import-export differential (export minus import) was US＄155. 14 billion, US＄26. 37 billion less than 2010. The figure continued to narrow 14. 5% on the basis of the 7. 2% gap compared with 2010.

In 2011, China's foreign trade mode and structure continued to improve. General trade resumed in strength, and the difference widened. Processing trade total and surplus grew by about 13%, and service trade grew steadily.

General trade import and export amounted to US＄1,924. 59 billion, an increase of 29. 2%, accounting for 52. 8% of China's total import-export value, and this percentage was 2. 7% higher than 2010. Out

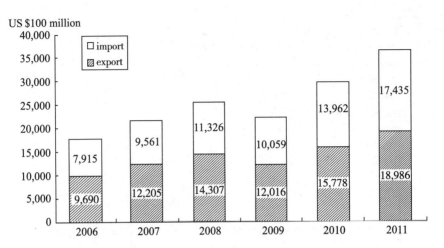

Figure 1.3 In recent years, China's commodities import and export continue to grow gradually to achieve balance

Source: National Bureau of Statistics of China, "2011 National Economic and Social Development Statistics".

of this, exports amounted to US $917.12 billion, an increase of 27.3% and 7% higher than the previous year in terms of total exports. Imports amounted to US $1,007.47 billion, an increase of 31%, and 6.1% higher than the previous year in terms of total imports. General trade items showed a negative difference of US $90.35 billion, widening the gap by 85.8%.

Processing trade import and export amounted to US $1,305.21 billion, an increase of 12.7%. Exports amounted to US $835.42 billion, an increase of 12.9%, while imports amounted to US $469.79 billion, an increase of 12.5%. The surplus under value-added trade was US $365.63 billion, an increase of 13.4%.

Service exports continued on the growth trend, with total imports and exports exceeding US $400 billion for the first time, setting a historical record. Exports and imports continued to rank among the world's highest numbers, occupying 4th and 3rd places respectively.

In 2011, China's foreign trade partners grew in diversity. Growth in trade with traditional markets of Europe, US and Japan was steady, while the growth in trade with new markets was even stronger (See

Table 1. 2).

China-European trade amounted to US $ 567. 21 billion, an increase of 18. 3%, but in terms of growth rate, it was 4. 2% lower than the growth in total import and export over the same period in China. China-US trade amounted to US $ 446. 65 billion, an increase of 15. 9%, and 6. 6% lower than the growth in total import and export in China over the same period. China-Japan trade amounted to US $ 342. 89 billion, an increase of 15. 1%, and 7. 4% lower than the growth in total import and export in China over the same period.

China's trade with ASEAN countries amounted to US $ 362. 85 billion, an increase of 23. 9%, and 1. 4% higher than the growth in import and export in China over the same period. Export to ASEAN countries was US $ 170. 08 billion, an increase of 23. 1%. Import from ASEAN countries was US $ 192. 77 billion, an increase of 24. 6%. The negative difference in trade with ASEAN countries was US $ 22. 69 billion, an expansion of 37. 1%.

Total import and export between China and Brazil, Russia and South Africa amounted to US $ 84. 2 billion, US $ 79. 25 billion and US $ 45. 43 billion respectively, an increase of 34. 5%, 42. 7% and 76. 7% respectively. These were all higher than China's total import and export growth, indicating that trade growth was strong in China's trade with new and developing countries.

Table 1. 2　In 2011, China's "fist" (main) products exported maintained an export growth rate of 15%~20% (US $ 100 million, %)

Category	Electric Products			Traditional Bulk Commodities		
	Overall	Electric and Electronic Products	Mechanical Equipment	Garment	Textiles	Shoes
Amount	10,855. 9	4,457. 9	3,537. 7	1,532. 2	946. 7	417. 2
Growth Rate	16. 3	14. 7	14. 2	18. 3	22. 9	17. 1

Source: Data from China Customs.

According to statistics from the Chinese Ministry of Commerce, in the first half of 2012, China's total imports and exports amounted to US $ 1, 839. 84 billion, an increase of 8%. Exports amounted to US

＄954.38 billion, an increase of 9.2%. Imports amounted to US ＄885.46 billion, an increase of 6.7%. From the responses from various parties at the G20 Summit in Mexico, we can see that China's foreign trade balance is progressively gaining recognition from the international community. A horizontal comparison with its trading partners shows that China's foreign trade development is quite good, with very few zero or negative growth with other countries. It is evident that China can still hope to achieve the 10% growth for the entire year.

In parallel with the slackening growth, China's foreign trade has exhibited some positive changes. For instance, if we observe the data on China's shoes exports, we can see that the export amount showed little growth, but the value of the exports was increasing. This shows that China-made shoes are moving from low-end products to high-end products. In other words, China's trade conditions are improving. Also, we can see that more and more traditional enterprises are determined to strengthen their research and development to enhance their product positioning and their competitiveness in the market.

In May 2012, in the factory of Zhejiang Qingmao Textile Printing and Dyeing Co., Ltd in Pujiang, Shaoqing, Zhejiang, production was full steam ahead. Although the time was not yet the prime season, the company's total exports in the first five months of the year was already 19.5% higher than the same period in the previous year. In recent years, with the appreciation of the RMB and the sustainable rise in labour costs, China is losing its competitive edge against countries like India and Vietnam in terms of the prices of textile products. As the traditional pillar industry in Zhejiang's foreign trade, the labour-intensive textile printing and dyeing industry is still facing a lack of overseas demand. So what made Qingmao Textile so busy?

"This must be attributed to our accurate market positioning and sustainable research and development." the Company's General Manager Xu Jianfeng said. Qingmao Textile invested heavily on research and development, and developed textiles that were water proof, stain proof, grease proof, and non-combustible. While ordinary cotton textiles fetched about US ＄1.5 per metre, the improved fire-proof textiles could fetch US $ 4 to US $ 5.

In 2011, China's non-financial industries actually utilized US $ 116 billion of FDI funds, an increase of 9. 7%. The annual non-financial direct foreign investment amounted to US $ 60. 1 billion, an increase of 1. 8% over 2010. Localisation is the best form of globalisation, and this has become a core value for Chinese enterprises that have multinational operations. One Chinese entrepreneur has said, "If you are serious about settling in another country, you have to integrate with this country. You cannot give people the impression that once you have made your money, you will leave. If you aim for quick money, you will not go anywhere. "

A lot of Chinese companies selling to overseas countries have localised their workforce. In their branch companies in Europe, US and Japan, the staff from salespersons to chief executives are all local people. According to statistics, for Chinese companies in the US, for every 10 jobs created in China, they will create 15 jobs in the US.

At the end of 2011, China's foreign exchange reserves exceeded US $ 3,000 billion to reach US $ 3,181. 1 billion, an increase of US $ 333. 8 billion compared with late 2010. At the end of 2011, the RMB exchange rate was RMB 6. 300 9 to US $ 1, an appreciation of 5. 1% compared with the end of 2010. On 21 June 2011, the central bank of China promulgated the "Notice on Related Issues on Cross Boundary RMB Businesses", officially laying out the pilot methods for foreign businesses that directly invest in the business of RMB clearing. This became an important measure in promoting RMB cross-border circulation.

According to the "Global Competitiveness Report 2010—2011" released by World Economic Forum, China's ranking in terms of competitiveness rose from rank 29 to rank 27. As the only country in the four BRICS countries registering a rise in ranking, China deserves recognition as the most competitive and vibrant emerging economy in the global economic arena.

From "Imitation" to "Innovation": Transformation of China's Industry Structure

Industry is the pillar of a country's economy. From its reform and opening-up to its accession to WTO, from its integration into the international arena to its rise in international competitions, China's industries have conquered numerous obstacles, won battles, and achieved enviable results. This shows that China's industry structure has always been in a state of dynamic adjustment.

In 2005, the world finally recognised China's car industry. From about 100 spare parts product radio sets produced in 1985 to about 1,000 spare parts product TV sets produced in 1995, and then about 10,000 spare parts product cars are being produced. This is the realisation of the dream of several generations. China is driving into the car society in two directions: the cars running on Chinese roads are all "cars made world-wide", while Chinese-made cars on other countries' roads are increasing in number.

On the one hand, China's car market is a highly international one, and imported cars are developing in the long term—from 50,000 cars in 2001 to 770,000 cars in 2010. On the other hand, cars made in China have not only withstood the impact of imported cars, but they have actually captured the international market. For Chinese national brand cars, only 180,000 were produced in 2008, but two years later—in 2010, the number increased to 3.63 million. In 2005, a surplus appeared for the first time in China's car trade. In 2001, Chery exported 10 cars to Syria, putting an end to the era of zero export for China-made cars. Since then, Chinese cars have been exported to Iran, Cuba, Malaysia and the US. Following the export of 2,000 Great Wall Haval （长城哈弗）H5 to the European Union in June 2010, 593 Great Wall Haval SUV and Great Wall Wingle （长城风骏皮卡）were exported to another high-end market—Australia—in September 2010.

When China entered into WTO, the country produced only 2 million cars. At that time, China was the only country in the world where goods vehicles outnumbered passenger vehicles. In 2009, China produced 13.791 million cars and sold 13.6448 million of them, for the first time exceeding 10 million cars, instantly becoming the world's number one car producing and car selling country. In 2010, when the world economy was still recovering from the financial crisis, China's volume of cars manufactured and sold increased by 32% against the previous year, exceeding the 18 million mark and retaining its position as world No. 1 (See Figure 1. 4). Among the cars produced, passenger vehicles were over three times that of commercial vehicles. In that year, China's car production accounted for 23.5% of global production, a dramatic increase from 3.5% in 2000. Meanwhile, China's car exports exceeded US$50 billion, of which the export of spares and parts accounted for over US$40 billion—78% of the total export of car commodities.

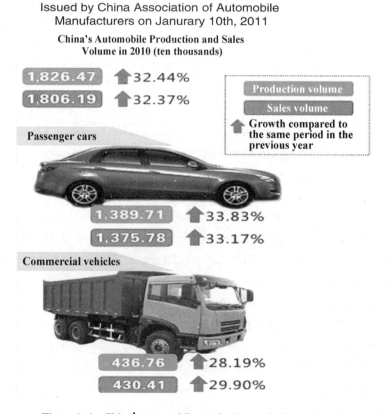

Issued by China Association of Automobile Manufacturers on Janurary 10th, 2011

China's Automobile Production and Sales Volume in 2010 (ten thousands)

Figure 1. 4   China's automobile production and sales volume in 2010 was ranked top 1 in the world

According to statistics from the China Association of Automobile Manufacturers, in 2011, although the domestic demand of cars in China were under restrictions for different reasons as traffic jam and the demand slowed down, yet export of cars still maintained its rapid growth.

In that year, the export of various types of cars numbered 814,300, an increase of 49.95% over the same period in the previous year, and 269,400 more than the previous year. This set a new historical record. This contributed as much as 60.79% over the same period. Of these, 476,100 were passenger cars for export. This was an increase of 269,400 over thesame period. Passenger cars exported numbered 338,200, an increase of 29.12%.

In the first half of 2012, the export of China's national brand cars amounted to 487,900, an increase of 28% over the same period last year. Of these, the export in May and June each exceeded 100,000 cars. Historical records were broken in the months of April, May and June continuously. Great Wall cars' exports to Southeast Asia and the Middle East are on the increase, while the two major China national brands Chery and Geely were far ahead of the average in size—exceeding 10,000 cars in June. In the first half of 2012, the total car sales in China were 9.6 million. If the macro economic situation in the latter half of the year takes a turn for the better, people can look forward to an 8% increase in performance, and breaking through the level of 20 million in sales.

Since its accession to WTO, another important industry of China—information technology production—is also on the rise. According to statistics, from 2001 to 2010, the production of IT products was on the rapid rise. In 2010, China's production of mobile phones, colour TV, personal computers and digital cameras crowned the world. The total import and export of electronic information products increased from US $124.1 billion in 2001 to US $1,012.8 billion in 2011, accounting for over 30% of China's total trade imports. Exports soared from US $65.02 billion in the past to US $591.2 billion, representing an annual increase of 27.8%.

China has enjoyed constant breakthroughs in researching into electronics and information technology. This has exemplified how this research permeates into the national economy and achieves a motivational effect. During the 11th Five-year Plan, the important project in information technology created an array of innovative products that own autonomous intellectual property. The computer systems of Dawning

5000A，Lenovo Shenteng 7000 and "Tianhe-1A" all achieved success，and maintained and even enhanced China's leadership status in developing high power computers. On the Tianhe-1A computer system，the China-made Central Processing Unit (CPU) FT-1000 finds verification and application. In the meantime，the project on integrated circuit equipment "65 nm Dielectric Etching machine" has already been sold in China，and has received orders from overseas.

　　If Americans excel at creation，then the Chinese have a competitive edge in innovation. Everyone has an equal chance to apply his intelligence. In the age of online information，whether it be ethnic Chinese brought up in the Western world，or professionals serving overseas enterprises in China，we can assert that in the development of various e-conomies，Chinese high-tech professionals have achieved superb research results. China is completely capable of autonomously developing its pool of high calibre talents. With the injection of capital and technological policy support，China is in an excellent position to rise to the very top on the global highway of information technology. China can，from a side angle，ride on the pulse of global scientific and economic development，and lay the foundation for the transformation from "muscle-labour" economy to "intellectual-labour consolidation" and "intellectual economy" (See Figure 1.5).

**Figure 1.5　Capital and policies lend support to the development of
new industries in information, biology and energy**

　　The fact is also just this. In the realm of communications and network technology, China is either catching up with, or trying to overtake the world. Following the introduction of the TD-SCDMA at the Beijing Olympics in 2008, China has successfully commercialised this system. Meanwhile, TD-LTE-Advanced, which owns autonomous intellectual property, has become a candidate for the 4th generation standard. Then the successful launch of the IEC61784-2/CPF14 has secured for China the enviable right of speech on the stage of international standardisation, which is dominated by the developed countries.

According to the "2011 Statistics on the Electronic Information Industry" released by the Ministry of Industry and Information Technology, the total imports and exports of electronic information products in 2011 totalled US $1,129. 23 billion, accounting for 31% of China's foreign trade imports and exports. The three major exports were: notebook computers (US $105. 88 billion), with an increase of 11. 1%; mobile phones (US $62. 76 billion), with an increase of 34. 3%; and integrated circuits (US $32. 57 billion), with an increase of 11. 4%. Revenue from the Chinese software industry accounted for over 15% of the global total. China's production of electronic products such as colour TV sets, mobile phones and computers accounted for 48. 8%, 70. 6% and 90. 6% respectively of the global production volume—achieving top global ranking on all fronts.

As the world's largest brand for home appliances, the Haier Group commands an 8% global market share. In the first half of 2012, China exported 42. 2 million mobile phones to the US, an increase of 21. 3% over the same period in the previous year, and an 80. 9% increase in dollar terms. Meanwhile, China exported 43. 9 million mobile phones to the European Union, an increase of 26. 8% over the same period in the previous year. Due to the relatively low baseline in 2011 and other entrepot factors, China's exports to the European Union achieved an increase of 156% over the same period in the previous year. In 2011, China exported US $229. 39 billion worth of computers, maintaining a growth rate of 5. 6%.

On the list of Global Top 500 Enterprises, there are 54 Chinese enterprises, 43 more than that of 2001. Of these Chinese enterprises, 30 are central government-owned enterprises, with Sinopec, State Grid Company of China (SGCC) and PetroChina among the top 10. Among the Global Top 500 Enterprises in 2012, Mainland China (including Hong Kong but not including Taiwan) companies continued the increasing trend for the 9th year running, with 73 companies on the list, with 12 new additions such as Geely compared with 2011. If we include Taiwan, then China has a total of 79 companies on the list. Indeed the number of Mainland China companies on the list has overtaken Japan, and is second only to the US, which is with 132 companies.

After accumulating several years of experience, China is now in a strong position to go overseas to do "bottom fishing" (抄底). The 2011 "Yellow Paper on World Economics" released by Chinese Academy of Social Sciences (CASS) stated that Chinese enterprises are changing roles—from companies being acquired, to companies acquiring assets. In 2010, the amount of acquisitions and mergers was ranked No. 2 in the world, second only to the US.

From "Out" to "In": Chinese Economic Blood Line Began to Present to World Supply Network

China's development cannot be isolated from the world. Since the late 1970s, multinational corporations from Japan, Europe and the US have been landing in China, bringing with them capital, advanced technology and management experience. This not only played a critical part in motivating the technological progress of Chinese enterprises, but it also opened the door for China in acquiring nutrition from the global economy.

The export markets and import sources for Chinese corporations have become more diversified. On the one hand, this provided an outlet for the nearly saturated production capacity in many places, and on the other hand, it boosted the energy supply for the middle and latter stage in the process of industrialisation. The absorption of Chinese export commodities in the world market has alleviated the unbalanced supply-demand in the Chinese domestic market, increasing the income for Chinese people in urban and rural areas, promoted employment, and enhanced social stability.

The imports from various economies in the world has alleviated the inadequacy of China's own resources, and safeguarded the huge demand for resources, energy and raw materials for the rapid growth of China's economy. Since 1993, China has been a net importing country for petroleum. In 2009, China imported 125. 834 million tons of coal, an increase of 211. 9% over the previous year. Meanwhile, China exported 22. 4 million tons of coal, a 50. 7% drop over the previous year. This made China a net importer of coal, with a net import of 10,300 tons. In recent years, with the discovery of new gas fields and with technological development, China's production of natural gas has been on the increase year by year. However, this has still not been able to catch up with the fast increasing domestic demand. According to the data released by the National Development and Reform Commission, the production of natural gas from January to May 2012 has increased by 7. 3% over the same period in the previous year. Meanwhile, the consumption of natural gas has increased by 15. 9% over the same period in the previous year, with an import of 16. 3 billion cubic metres of natural gas—an increase of 42. 8%.

The integration of the regional economy has enhanced the welfare of Chinese producers and consumers. The streamlining of customs procedures and the coordination of management have lowered the transaction costs and enhanced the efficiency of trade as well as boosted the profits of export enterprises. Now, consumers are able to directly feel the benefits brought by product diversification and the convenience of choice. For instance, with the establishment of the China-ASEAN Free Trade Area (CAFTA), people in Nanning can buy from the various supermarkets a great variety of fruits and foods—Garsinia mangostana from Thailand, dried mangos from the Philippines, golden cakes from Indonesia and dried pineapples from Vietnam. Beijing residents can now buy fresher tropic fruits like durian. In short, the special produces from ASEAN countries are now available over a short time in different parts of China.

Not only is the trading of commodities and services nurturing the economic growth of China, the international circulation of other essential factors are important channels for the global economy to permeate into the Chinese economic system. The increased movement of Chinese labour has motivated the international exchange and improvement of technology, and also promoted the improvement of the quality of the workforce and the optimisation of the industrial structure. In 2011, 190,000 Chinese citizens returned to China after furthering their studies abroad—an increase of 38% over the previous year. In recent years, Chinese enterprises have been eager to "go out" and map out strategies for the "two markets" —the Chinese domestic market and the international market. They actively coordinate the "two resources" within and outside China, enhancing the efficiency of resource allocation, and effectively steered clear of some of the trade barriers.

As a large developing country without a strong foundation, China definitely gained a lot from its participation in the global economy. However, economic globalisation is a rapier (double-edged sword) to any country, and China is no exception. For instance, as export-oriented economies rely on exports, domestic employment is more prone to the impact of changes in the economic environment. In the summer of 2012, the flux of labourers back to their home town—a phenomenon that used to appear before the Chinese New Year—already occurred. This is related not only to the control of real estate and the structural adjustments in the domestic and overseas economies, but also to the slackened demand in the traditional US and European markets, the critical situation in foreign trade that caused a declined demand in labour in foreign enterprises. Indeed, as the saying goes, water that bears the boat is the same that swallows it up.

Another example is that a prolonged period of foreign trade surplus has become a source of domestic inflation in China. With the increase in foreign exchange reserves, the Central Bank needs to maintain the fundamental stability of the RMB exchange rate and suppress the appreciation of the exchange rate. Hence it is obliged to issue basic money to buy in these foreign exchanges. Although the Central Bank can issue notes for hedging, yet an increase in liquidity is inevitable. And in the increase in foreign exchange reserve, a surplus in foreign trade is an important component.

Another example is that various economies in the world are increasingly concerned about the environmental issues in China as a rising large developing country. To protect the environment while ensuring economic growth, we must on the one hand reduce the existing pollutants brought by prolonged economic development, and on the other hand control the new pollutants expected to be emitted as a result of economic development. Hence China is facing greater and greater pressure in protecting the environment in the course of its economic development.

The China Factor in Globalisation

Pulling Agent: Demands from China Boosting Global Growth

In 2010, China and Japan each accounted for about 9% of the global economy. At the same time, the 27 countries under the European Union accounted for over one quarter, and the US alone accounted for another quarter. This is the production pattern in the global economy. In the world today, the overall contribution of the US, European Union and Japan to the global economy is apparent, and China's growing contribution is irreplaceable. Hence the traditional "three pillars" have become less powerful as a positive pull in the global economy (See Figure 1. 6).

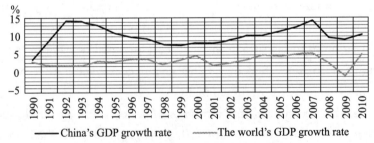

————China's GDP growth rate --------The world's GDP growth rate

Figure 1. 6 China has for many years been an important pulling force in the growth of the world economy

Source: Data about China from 1990 to 2008 come from *China Statistical Yearbook 2010*. In 2009 and 2012, China's GDP increased 9. 2% and 10. 4% respectively, and this was confirmed as the audited figures released by the National Statistics Bureau of China on 11 January 2011 and 10 January 2012. The data about the world come from *World Economic Outlook Database*, September 2011, IMF.

China has become an important force contributing to the steady growth of the global economy. In the modern world, there has not been any large economy that can maintain an annual growth rate of 7% for 40 years, except China. From 2003 to 2006, China maintained a double-digit growth each year, with an average annual growth rate of 10. 4%, more than double that of the world average of 4. 9%.

Statistics from the World Bank indicates that in 2003, China's contribution to the newly increased global GDP growth was 4. 6%. This figure increased to 14. 5% in 2009, making China the top contributor to global GDP growth newly increased. From 2001 to 2010, China's GDP grew by US $ 4,600 billion, accounting for 14. 7% of the global economic newly increased value over the same period.

Meanwhile, China's contribution to the absolute value of the GDP has also been on the constant increase. It has risen from 1. 7% in 1980 to 4. 4% in 2002, 5. 5% in 2006, and 9. 3% in 2010 (See Table 1. 3). According to Goldman Sachs' research data, China's accumulated contribution to the global economy from 2000 to 2009 has exceeded 20%, overtaking the US.

Table 1. 3　　**Over the past 30 years, China has been increasingly contributing to the world's key economic indicators** (%)

Indicator	1980	1990	2000	2007	2008	2009
GDP	1. 7	1. 6	3. 8	6. 2	7. 1	8. 6
Total imports and exports	0. 9	1. 6	3. 6	7. 7	7. 9	8. 8
Exports	0. 9	1. 8	3. 9	8. 7	8. 9	9. 6
Imports	1. 0	1. 5	3. 3	6. 7	6. 9	7. 9
Direct foreign investments	0. 1	1. 7	3. 0	4. 2	6. 4	8. 5

Source: World Bank, World Development Indicator Database; IMF Database.

WTO data shows that from 2000 to 2009, China's import and export trade volumes increased at an annual rate of 17% and 15% respectively, far higher than the global trade volume of 3% over the same period. During the period of the 11th Five-year Plan (2006 to 2010), China's import-export trade total volume increased at an average annual rate of 15. 9%, higher than the growth in global trade over the same period.

In 2009, when the impact of the international financial crisis was at its worst, and against the background of a 12.9% decline in global trade, China's import volume still exceeded US $ 1,000 billion, becoming the world's second largest importing country, and the only country among the major economies to register growth. Hence China has made significant contribution to the global economic recovery.

Today, about 35% of the GDP of the various economies in the world are directly participating in exchanges at different levels in the global economy, and essential elements in manufacturing are extensively circulating around the world. To optimise the allocation of resources like capital, information, technology and manpower in the global context, it is essential that there is deepening dependency among various economies. In terms of dependence on foreign trade, it is about 30% for the US, Japan, India and Brazil, less than 50% for France, UK, Italy and Russia, and over 50% for China, Canada and Germany. China's own economic vitality will be transmitted to other economies in the world through a variety of channels and in a diversity of methods.

Having entered into WTO for more than a decade, Chinese commodities are moving out to the world, and commodities from other countries are starting to enter China through the increasingly mature trade channels. While the world's attention is focused mostly on China's exports, a lot of people are not aware that China is also a large importing country.

In 2000, China was the world's 7th largest exporting country and and 8th largest importing country. Now, China has grown into the world's largest exporting country and second largest importing country. Indeed, China's import has in the past decade been increasing at an annual average rate of 20%.

Among China's top 10 trade partners in 2010, apart from Taiwan of China and Brazil, China's import growth rates from these trade partners were all higher than the export growth rates. The demands for China's 1.34 billion people are profound, diversified, and sustained. At present, China has become the top export market for Japan, Australia, Brazil and South Africa, the second top export market for the European

Union, and the third top export market for the US.

As the fastest growing economy globally, China has become the world's largest absorber of resources. At present, China is importing over 56% of its crude oil, natural gas and iron ore consumed. Meanwhile, the import of natural resources needed to maintain its fast growth is accounting for over 35% of its consumption. This remains an important source of export income for economies that thrive on their own natural resources.

Take the iron and steel industry as an example. China's economy has experienced a process of rapid growth, and the huge amount of infrastructure and real estates developments have provided China's iron and steel industry with valuable development opportunities. Accompanying the development of the iron and steel industry, the trading of iron ore has entered its phase of rapid growth. 10 years ago, China imported only 92.3 million tons of iron ore. The volume increased to 100 million tons in 2002, 200 million tons in 2004, and 400 million tons in 2008. In 2011, the import volume reached 600 million tons. As the world's largest iron and steel manufacturing country, China also became the world's largest importer of iron ore.

The increase in China's import volume has pulled up the price of iron ore. Not only had its price risen to US $200 per ton, iron ore had once become a "rare and valuable" commodity. Now when Chinese businessmen go to countries like Australia and Canada for business negotiations, the people there are very friendly, because they are able to feel that China's demand is crucial to the development of their own national economy. This was particularly true in 2008, when prices of iron ore plunged drastically under the impact of the world economic crisis. And due to the launch of China's policies to stimulate economic growth, China's iron and steel industry became the first industry to recover. This in turn boosted the economic recovery of ore producing countries like Australia, Canada and Brazil.

China's demand was to a large extent influenced the supply-demand relationship and commodity pricing in the international market. Such was the case with iron ore, and such was the case with many other commodities. This kind of demand originates from the rapid development of the China economy, and it also stimulates the economic growth of commodity exporting countries. For many imported raw materials, after being processed in China, they become commodities for export to other markets around the world. Indeed, the Chinese economy and the global economy are mutually dependent and mutually beneficial in the flow and circulation of commodities.

Accompanying the increase in income for Chinese citizens, the import of consumer products into China is clearly on the rise. In Chinese towns, cars, electronic products and travel and leisure packages have become an important pulling factor for economic growth. Private planes and private boats have become consumer goods in China too. In less than 20 years, luxury goods have been imported into China in large volumes—their high prices have not scared away people who have no idea what the brands mean, but they have lured these people into a buying spree. According to a report released by the World Association for Luxury Goods Consumption in January 2012, at the end of December 2011, China's market for luxury goods has grown to an annual size of US \$ 12. 6 billion (not including private planes, leisure boats and luxury cars), accounting for 28% of the global volume. China has become the world's largest consuming nation for luxury goods.

At the same time, more and more Chinese are travelling and spending overseas. Up to the end of 2011, China has approved 140 countries or regions as tourism destinations for their citizens, with 111 of them actually being implemented. During the period of 11th Five-year Plan, the markets of domestic tourism, inbound travel and outbound travel all prospered, making China the world's third largest host country for inbound travellers and source of outbound travellers. Indeed, the tourism industry has entered a new phase of popular style and industrialisation.

Prior to the London 2012 Olympics, the British Government launched excessive publicity and exaggerated the boosting power of the Olympics on Britain's tourism industry. This signal made some businesses increase their prices or increase their supply, resulting in a tragic over-supply. However, the Chinese tourists and consumers became the highlight of Britain's Olympics tourism market. In the first week, the average expenditure of Chinese tourists topped the list of consumers all over the world. The average spending for each Chinese traveller was as high as 203 pounds, nearly 10% higher than the second, the United Arab Emirates. Indeed, the spending of Chinese tourists was in line with the number of medals that the Chinese athletes amassed. The Mayor of London, Boris Johnson, should indeed present a "champion spender" medal to the Chinese tourists.

Although the spending power of the post-1980 and post-1990 born migrant labors in China cannot be compared with the big spenders in cities and towns, yet they will become the main powerhouse in China's social and economic development. At present, the new generation of migrant workers number approximately 100 million, about 60% of China's migrant working population. In contrast with the older generation of migrant workers, the new generation live a more urban life, with newer concepts of consumption. This has boosted the growing demand for online electronic consumer goods. With their progressively growing income, they are a group of consumers not to be neglected—whether they eventually choose to merge with the wave of urbanisation, or to purchase property back in their home town.

In the western and vast inner land parts of China are vast areas of poor and underdeveloped regions. The Western "Triangular region" formed by linking together the cities of Chongqing, Chengdu and Xi'an will become China's fourth economic zone, after the Yangtze River Delta, Pearl River Delta and the Beijing-Tianjin-Hebei Triangular region. The development and transformation of these areas will take considerable time for construction and investment, and require great potential room for sustainable development. For a long time, China's export for foreign trade had taken the form of "strong in the east and weak in the west", and the 11 provinces in the east once accounted for over 90% of the total exports. Against the background of the eastern provinces slackening their export activities, a lot of regions in the west are actively developing their export economies. Coupled with the trend of processing trades moving towards the west, the western part of China can provide new dynamics to China's foreign imports and exports.

In July 2012, a lot of western provinces in China boasted eye-opening interim reports. The western areas' economic growth rate of over 10% may become a new engine of power for China to drive the global economic growth forward. In the first half of 2012, the income growth for urban and rural residents in the western provinces were in general higher or close to their GDP growth rate, and this is one of the attractions in the economic operations of western China.

A lot of multinational corporations do not take heed of the views of the pessimists, and are charging ahead in their investments in China's western provinces and cities—they believe in the huge market development potentials of western China.

Manufacturing Agent: Chinese Exports Provide Convenience to Global Markets

The rule of WTO is to encourage market competition. From "purchasing Chinese products" to "buying and selling global commodities", a lot of overseas businessmen have noticed the positive effects of China's accession to WTO, and hope to achieve all-win situations through "buying and selling global commodities". In the last decade or so, consumers all over the world have gradually come to realise that "Made in China" does not mean lowering prices to boost sales, but to produce on demand, and value for money.

In that year, Mr Mu Qizhong of the Nande Group successfully completed the largest single barter trade in the history of Chinese-Russian trade—using 800 truckloads of daily necessities and light products from over 300 factories to exchange for 4 Ty-154M aeroplanes. This legendary transaction is still being talked about today. A lot of countries like to buy small commodities made in China. For instance, light industries have always been a weak spot in Russia, and Chinese commodities are therefore in a very good position to support this "shorter leg". Indeed, globalised economy puts this division of labour into practice.

If you take a casual stroll in one of the shopping centres or supermarkets in the US, you will notice that almost all the clothing, whether or not of international brand, is made in China. In the last decade, China-made products have been on the increase—like inflating a balloon. "Made in China" is like a shadow that appears in the daily life of any ordinary American—from the clothing one puts on in the morning, the briefcase for work or going on trip, the office equipment, the electronic products for leisure use, the cooking utensils for dinner, the toys for the kids, the shoes for taking a walk, to the desk lamp and the alarm clock—are all "Made in China".

This is especially true as Christmas approaches—no matter it is the skating shoes that the kids want, or the Christmas tree for the family, and even the great variety of gift packs—are almost without exception "Made in China". Most Americans are very practical—they take no heed of the place of manufacturing—all they care about is whether the goods meet their needs in life, and whether they are value for money and are aligned with their income level.

Facts prove that choosing "Made in China" products can save a lot of money for the Americans. As we mentioned earlier, data from the US Chinese Embassy show that in the past decade China-made products have saved as much as US$600 billion. The research stated that "Made in China" has given each US family US$1,000 a year as disposable income.

At present, the US manufacturing industry is facing the "hollowing out phenomenon". Apart from some high-tech products, most of the commodities are being contracted out overseas for production, in order to save costs. As "Made in USA" products get fewer and fewer, some Americans are starting to get worried. CNBC once did a TV documentary—an elderly American lady tried her very best to support US products. She did not mind the cost—as long as a product is "Made in USA", she would buy it. The result was that to complete one round of daily purchase she would have to visit many places by car to buy all the things she needed. In general, most of the Americans are more than happy to choose the economical "Made in China" goods. After all, not everyone can afford to buy US-made products that are two to three times more expensive. One Harvard professor once said that "Made in China" has promoted the growth of the US economy, and made a positive impact on keeping inflation under control.

"Made in China" has brought good news to consumers—not only in developed countries, but consumers in ASEAN countries have noticed the benefits as they trade with China. For instance, residents in Kuala Lumpur, Malaysia can now buy even cheaper TV sets. In Hanoi, Vietnam, if you visit the shops, supermarkets and large commercial centres, you will find that a lot of quality Chinese products, from knitting kit to domestic electric appliances, are on the shelves. This has provided to the Vietnamese people more economical and more diversified products. In Thailand, the industries of agriculture, fishery, timber, rubber and electronics have all benefited from the establishment and implementation of CAFTA. As a result, the prices of many products have fallen. In Indonesia, the people at first feared the influx of large volumes of Chinese goods. They even demanded that the Government defer the implementation of the Free Trade Zone. Now they have changed their stand and started to support the establishment of the Free Trade Zone.

Admittedly copycat mobile phones comprise a grey area, yet for some countries in Africa and the South Asia, if there are no low price copycat mobile phones, their people would have to defer their purchase of mobile phones for a considerable time. In fact, the copycat mobile phones are not just an imitation of famous brands of mobile phones. They also demonstrate their special creativity in terms of technological design, look and feel, as well as their functions. Just after Barack Obama was elected US President, there appeared in Kenya a mobile phone advertisement with a fake Obama image as the spokesperson. According to data from the Indian Mobile Phone Association, since 2007, the brandless mobile phones have seen exponential growth in numbers. There were less than 5.5 million such mobile phones in 2007—2008; in 2009—2010 the number shot up to 20 million, and in 2011 the number reached 38 million.

Consumer: Chinese Market Attracts Multinational Corporations

For foreign enterprises operating in China, they have remitted a total of US $261.7 billion from 2001 to 2010, with an average annual growth of 30%. On this wonderful piece of land that is China, multinational corporations from all industries and from all countries have shown great vitality and energy.

People regard food as their prime want. The Chinese people, no matter rich or poor, all enjoy the pleasure of taste. Coca-Cola's popularity in China is no difference from any other place in the world. At a new product mark announcement hosted by Starbucks in March 2011, their Managing Director for China—Wang Jinlong—said that the success of Starbucks was closely tied with their development in China since 1999, and the company's development in China in the next four decades would depend on China. For KFC, their 3,000 shops are all successful and profitable. On top of this, KFC China is even painting the smile of Colonel Sandoz on the landscape of some four-tier cities. This is in sharp contrast to their decline (and some of the chain restaurants have even closed down) in the US, where they came from. As the market with the fastest growth rate in terms of new restaurant openings, China has become the third largest market globally for McDonald's. The company forecast that in 2012, their investment in China would be 50% more than that of the previous year. About 250 new restaurants will be opened during the year. Meanwhile, car-restaurant "Drive-Through" will be one of the focuses of development in the project.

In the realm of garment, the spending power of the middle income group in China is rapidly on the rise. According to the Bloomberg Billionaire Index, with the stock price of ZARA's mother company Inditex SA setting a record high at market close on 8 August 2012, the company's 76-year-old founder—Amancia Ortega from Spain found his fortune gaining an extra US $ 1.6 billion, to reach US $ 46.6 billion, overtaking Warren Buffett, Managing Director of Berkshire Hathaway Inc. with a net fortune of US $ 45.7 billion. Ortega then became the world's third richest person. Since five months after the release of the Bloomberg Billionaire Index, Buffett had all along maintained his third position. However, two months ago Ortega beat the founder of IKEA—Ingvar Kamprad, with his fortune of US $ 37 billion, now the richest man in Europe.

While the domestic market in Spain has been unstable since the debt crisis, and the Government has been resisting the pressure to apply for assistance from the central bank of Europe, yet Ortega's personal wealth in 2012 shot up US＄11. 4 billion, an increase of up to 32％. So what is the trick used by the "fast-accomplished leader of the fashion kingdom" to acquire wealth? His path to fortune was to open new shops in newly industrialized markets like China. The huge consumer market of China's middle class has offered to ZARA an irreplaceable space for development. This was crucial to the 40-year-old company Inditex SA reaping a profit for 12 consecutive seasons.

In the realm of cars and electronics, the size of China's huge consumer market has made old companies very happy. In 2011, China made a trade deficit of US＄11. 7 billion—US＄1. 9 billion higher than 2010. This trade deficit was achieved through the import of car load. In the entire year of 2011, China imported a total of 1. 03 million entire cars, a growth of 28％ over the same period in the previous year. Driven by strong demand, General Motors Company sold more cars in China than in the US. As for BMW and Rolls-Royce, China has also become their largest market in the world for their luxury cars. Benz forecast that in 2015, China would overtake Germany and the US as their largest market in the world. Whenever Apple Corporation launches a new product, their outlets in China will need a team of security guards comparable in size to the police stationed at Madison Square when U2 gave their concert there. Judging from the volume of downloads of the application procedures of Apple iPhone and iPad, China has in 2011 become the second largest market globally for App Store, after the US.

The same scenario applies to the financial industry. Following China's accession to WTO a decade ago, China has constantly opened up its financial arena to allow more foreign capital companies to enter the China market. While foreign companies bring to the China market advanced management concepts and enriched financial services, they also benefit a lot from the rapid development of the Chinese economy.

Take the insurance industry as an example. In late 2004, the Chinese insurance industry ended its transitional period and took the lead in implementing the total opening-up of the financial industry. Over the decade, the over 40 overseas insurance companies listed among the Fortune 500 have entered into China's insurance market. As one of the 10 top insurance enterprises in the US, AIA Company that was originally set up in Shanghai, China, re-entered China in the early 1990s, and found new space for growth in the Chinese market. They were listed in Hong Kong in October 2010, becoming the greatest IPO in the history of Hong Kong.

Output Agent: Chinese Factor Supports Technology Innovation

All the significant milestones in the history of mankind are invariably linked with reforms in productivity. To develop the global economy, we can rely on consumption in the short term; but in the long term we must rely on innovation. China's export commodities are cheap and of good quality, and help to lower the cost of living for the consumers, as well as reduce the purchasing and production costs for the manufacturers all over the world. In the meantime, through greater competition they stimulate the technological advancement of the importing countries and indirectly promote innovation in the production process.

The outflow of high calibre talents from China indirectly raises the competitiveness of other countries' technology and industry. Developed countries like to move their processing work to China that has an abundance of manpower, so that they will be able to invest more manpower, materials and financials to develop new industries and continue to lead the world's economic trends. Today, when various districts in the world carry out research and development, they will notice a great difference and a lot of distinctions.

The US has made huge investments to conduct research into newly developed strategic industries. The focus of their innovation is on new sources of energy, and the ongoing research directions include corn alcohol, clean electricity generation, highly effective long distance power transmission, intelligent power grid, solar panels, and high efficiency fuel batteries. In February 2012, US Secretary for Energy Steven Chu announced that in the next five years, the US Government would invest US $ 120 million to set up a new energy innovation hub, to conduct research on advanced battery technology and energy storing technology.

In the financial year of 2012, the Government will allocate US $20 million mainly to expedite research into electro-chemical energy storage.

Europe's high-tech innovation puts relatively more focus on life sciences, and overall speaking, it lags behind the US. We will always remember that in 1997 the world's first cloned sheep Dolly, born in the Roslin Institute in Edinburgh, was a milestone breakthrough that shocked the world. The world's first batch of asexually reproduced genetically engineered sheep were also born in the UK. With the commissioning of the Life Sciences Laboratory Building in Stockholm, Sweden in May 2010, DNA sequencing work on European Picea started, with an aim to detect the genetic configuration of this kind of "Christmas tree" by 2013. European Picea is an evergreen coniferous plant often used as Christmas trees. As their wood is soft and the strands are straight, they are also used for building, as well as making furniture, musical instruments and boats. Sweden is using this laboratory to build the largest genetic centre in Europe, taking an unprecedented move in integrating genomics with proteomics.

Sony's Walkman has been hailed as Japan's greatest contribution to the 20th century. It once took the world by storm, taking the lead in enhancing the lifestyle of the younger generation. Although Japan's technological innovation has been criticised as "bringing the 21st century back to the 20th century", yet their robotic technology is still leading the world. In May 2010, a "companion robot" that can play the violin made its appearance in the Shanghai World Expo. In September of the same year, Chiba Industrial University developed "Core", a robot that can bend its knees and walk around, carrying loads of up to 96 kg. In October of the same year, the National Institute of Advanced Industrial Science and Technology and Osaka University jointly developed a robot that can simulate different facial expressions. Using a young lady as the prototype, the robot is connected to the computer camera, and after identifying the expressions of the operator, it can instruct the robot to put on the same expression.

While there is no single truth, truth is everywhere to be found. The focus of innovation for the emerging markets in the Asia Pacific is the electronic information industry. Although their high technologies are not yet at the cutting edge in the world, yet they are able to ride on the products' life cycles and gain cost advantage through large scale standardised production, or through the use of a powerful sales network as core competency to sell the products of other economies to the world. Indeed, their special core competitiveness has led the strong growth of their economy. In the US, Apple mobile phones are leading the fashion trend in electronic products. Meanwhile, Korea's Samsung and Taiwan's HTC have also created their own territory in the intelligent mobile phone market.

Contributor: The Rise of China Motivates Its Developing Partners

To the developing countries in Asia, Africa and Latin America, China is a "friendly giant". In East Asia, China is integrating into their production network, not to displace other developing economies from their opportunities for international division of work, but to promote the expansion of multinational corporations in East Asia to enhance the economic vibrancy in the region. Through the import of spare parts, China achieves supply chain cooperation, risk sharing, labour-intensive production and industry transfer, thus benefitting the East Asian econo-mies. This works against the rules of the zero-sum game theory.

Take ASEAN as an example. In October 2004, at the "Chinese Business Leaders Forum" organised by Chinese Enterprises (Singapore) Association, former ASEAN secretary general Mr Wang Jingrong point-ed out, "To ASEAN, the rise of China is not a threat, but a valuable opportunity for economic development... The ASEAN-China Free Trade Zone is an ingenious way to enable each party to realise its own goals."

China's need for raw materials, agricultural products, intermediate products and capital products provide ASEAN export enterprises with valuable business opportunities. In 2009, under the impact of the inter-national financial crisis, Malaysia's exports to the US, European Union and Japan dropped 27%, 19% and 23% respectively. On the other hand, its exports to China grew 6%. In the same year, Thailand's ex-ports to the US, European Union and Japan dropped 18%, 23% and

22% respectively, yet its exports to China dropped only 1%. In 2010, with the operation of CAFTA and benefitting from the implementation of "zero tariff", Thailand's exports to China increased about 30% over the previous year, and China can look forward to becoming Thailand's biggest export market. In the wholesale markets Sampheng Lane in Bangkok, Thailand, the purchase costs for the commodities have lowered thanks to the lower tariffs, and the income for the shop owners actually increased substantially.

Through global competition on commodities and essential factors, China is encouraging trade partner countries that are also in the developing world to implement related policies that stimulate the accumulation of human capital, so as to actively carry out production innovations and various internal reforms. Brazil, the largest country in Latin America, and the world's 6th largest economy, are leading Latin America in terms of technology and innovation. In the production of ethanol petrol, and in the utilisation of renewable energy, Brazil is among the top countries in the world. Multinational corporations have found that some of the products and technologies developed by Brazilians (such as cars, planes, software packages, optical fibre and electrical appliances) are rather competitive.

On 30 June 2011, INSEAD and the United Nations Intellectual Property Organisation jointly announced in Paris the 2011 Global Innovation Index rankings. Brazil's efforts in innovation has reaped significant results—their innovation index ranking rose from No. 60 in 2010 to No. 47 in 2011, even ahead of Russia, India and Argentina. China was ranked No. 29—on the top 30 list for the first time, a jump of 14 places compared with 2010.

In terms of capital and technology, China is actively rendering assistance to other economies. According to the "China's Assistance to Other Countries White Paper" published by the News Office of the State Council on 21 April 2011, up to the end of 2009, China has accumulatively rendered assistance to 161 countries and over 30 international and regional organisations, with 123 developing countries regularly receiving assistance from China. Cumulatively China has given out funds to external parties, amounting to RMB 256. 29 billion. Of these RMB 106. 2 billion was pure donations, RMB 76. 54 billion was interest-free loans, and RMB 73. 55 billion was in concessionary loans. China has also organised over 4,000 training courses in China for developing countries, deploying 120,000 trainer-sessions, including interns, managerial and technical staff, as well as officials. The over 20 types of training included economics, diplomacy, agriculture, healthcare and environmental protection. China has signed debt-exemption agreements with 50 countries in Africa, Asia, Latin America, the Carribean and Oceania. A total of 30 due debts were exempted, totalling RMB 25. 58 billion.

As the largest trade partner, China has invested in over 150 agricultural projects in Africa. Chinese investors look at Ethiopia—a country with very little mineral ores but has 9 million consumers—as a land full of opportunities. In the Kenyan capital of Nairobi, a lot of infrastructure—from the airport to housing project for low-income families—was constructed by China. In Mozambique, China has invested in building and maintaining industrial parks, and in setting up manufacturing centres in textiles and garments. In 2011, China's direct investments in Africa reached US＄13 billion, and bilateral trade amounted to US＄155 billion. Chinese enterprises are investing in Africa to improve the infrastructure and facilities there, and to promote the development of manufacturing departments.

China is maintaining a trade deficit with 48 of the least developed countries in the world, including Laos and Angola. Since 2008, China has been their largest export market. This not only assisted them in their economic development, but also actively contributed to the eradication of poverty in the world.

Part 2
Mechanism and Pattern

China Becomes the World Factory: "Passive" and "Active"

"Flying Geese Mode" and International Industry Transfer: "Flower Drum Transfer"

Since the 1960s, the economic runway of the East Asian region has been staging a relay of international industrial transfer. The participants, in chronological order, were: developed economies of Japan→newly industrialised economy, that is, Hong Kong of China, Korea, Singapore, Taiwan of China→four ASEAN countries, that is, Indonesia, Malaysia, the Philippines, Thailand→developing countries that are implementing opening-up strategy, such as China and Vietnam. In the "flying geese mode", characterised by the multi-layer industry transfer, the goose that spearheads the flight formation is Japan which, after the Second World War, snatched the title of "World Factory" from the US.

At the end of 1985, the Chinese Government relaxed its policy to attract foreign capital, and to encourage export-driven foreign enterprises to come to China to invest in factory building. Then Hong Kong and other economies entered China on a large scale. On the basis of the free flow of essentials and reasonable allocation, China continued to dynamically receive dynamic transfers from the world's advanced industries, and to realise the huge output growth. In the mid and late 1990s, Chinese citizens said goodbye to shortage, and they created unprecedented material wealth. Since the turn of the century, students of economics no longer (like their teachers) study the book *Shortage Economics*—a book on socialist economy by Hungarian economist Janos Kornai.

In 1997 and 1998, after the Asian financial crisis, China took over from Japan the role of "World Factory". In a way, China "reluctantly" became the World Factory. The Asian Financial Crisis messed up the outskirts of global finance, but the function of the world's financial centre—to allocate the world's resources—has not been harmed. They are still in demand, and still growing.

As the production lines of Southeast Asian economies have been hit hard, the orders from the US and Europe were directed to China. But at that time, China's production capacity was not sufficient to cope with the flood of order. So what happened? Wall Street and the City of London exercised the basic function of finance, and effectively allocated the global resources. The inflows of direct investments have brought along capital, equipment and technology. China had cheap land, labour, and environment to entice them; China had an extensive market, and in individual years the foreign capital coming to China exceeded that of the US and was ranked No. 1 in the world.

At that time, China's orders were from the US and Europe. China's production capacity was built with foreign capital. The red flower in the "flower drum transfer" game suddenly landed on China, and China became the new "world factory", which henceforth became an integral part of the global industry chain. China's newly acquired excess production capacity, the surplus of its current account, and the world's top foreign exchange reserve, all contributed to China's monopoly of the global allocation of capital resources.

For the development of China's economy itself, the fact that China was made the "world factory" was both a blessing and a reason for concern. The blessing is that China has more deeply penetrated into the gushing current of the global economy, with more jobs created, faster economic growth, upgrading of the industrial structure, better welfare for the producer and consumer, and the significantly higher salaries for the government, enterprises and residents. On the other hand, what was worrying was that China's road to trade imbalance was a journey of no return, and for a prolonged period China was stuck in the low value-added, high carbon-emitting position of low to medium end production. The product piloting, the production of key spare parts, as well as sales and after-sales service were all in the hands of developed countries; the production of modular spare parts was scattered over newly industrialised economies of Korea and Taiwan of China, and the packaging task, which offers little profit margin, was transferred to China.

The truth behind every phenomenon is usually surprising. For an Apple iPod player that has 451 spare parts, its retail price in the US is US $ 299, and the US local enterprises and workers reaped a maximum of US $ 163 in value added. This includes US $ 80 for Apple Corporation, US $ 75 for the distributors and retailers, and US $ 8 for the spare part manufacturer. Japan reaps an added value of US $ 26, and what China gets is only US $ 4 of processing fee. For every iPod exported to the US, China's trade surplus to the US would increase about US $ 150. The Chinese workers get only US $ 8 in income for every iPad computer, which is only 1.6% of the retail price. And for every iPad sold, Apple Corporation gets US $ 150, which is 30% of the retail price. Compared with Korea—where the main spares are produced—China's share of the profit was less than 1/4.

With China becoming the world's factory, trade between China and other economies will manifest a triangular trade pattern based on an industry chain division of labour. The production essentials, industrial structure and complementary situation have made the regional situation in the entire East Asia region a highly related system of international division of labour. In this system, apart from Hong Kong having a trade surplus, China's trade with different systems in Southeast Asia frequently experiences a trade deficit. China's trade with other economies such as the US and European Union countries has huge amounts of surplus in the current account. On the other hand, Southeast Asian economies' trading with China and other countries are all in surplus.

In other words, although China has become the largest export market for more and more East Asian developing economies, yet a large part of the imports from East Asian economies are used on consumer products exported to the US and European Union. It is estimated that for every US $ 100 of processed products exported to the US and the European Union, about US $ 35 to US $ 40 is contributing to the growth of East Asian economies. The pattern of global trade has become this—the capital products, spare parts and other complex intermediary products exported by East Asian economies are processed and assembled in China into finished products which are exported to US and European markets (See Figure 2. 1).

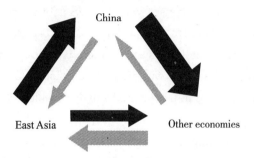

Figure 2. 1   Behind China's Overall Trade Surplus: Deficit Against East Asia

Note: The black arrows and the gray arrows represent trade surplus and deficit respectively. The width of the arrows is proportional to the size of the trade balance.

Compared with other economies, China, as the "world factory", has a unique kind of foreign export where processing trade accounts for up to half of the total. China is like a bakery—on the one hand, it imports flour, and adds in the necessary ingredients and labour cost, and bakes all sorts of bread. On the other hand, it exports cheap and delicious bread. This also reflects the simple truth that bread is more expensive than flour. The selling price of the end product must be higher than the raw materials. So it is only natural that China's processing trade will have a surplus.

We have all along been saying that in order to change the mode of foreign trade we must raise the added value of processing. But the higher the added value is, the higher the percentage of China's income from the selling price is, and therefore the higher the trade surplus is. This results in a conflict between the goal of "balancing trade" and the means of "raising the added value". In the meantime, the higher the value of the RMB is, the lower the price of the imported raw materials priced in RMB is, and the higher the price of the exported products is, and the higher the surplus of the processing trade is. In the current situation, it is only when the Chinese economy overheats, with more imported raw materials and primary products being used in domestic production departments rather than export production departments, that China will have a trade deficit.

"Wintelism" and the "Magnet Effect" of Global Production Network

After the modern mega industry was established in the second industrial revolution, the Western enterprises with the US as a representative implemented the Ford production mode, pushing the global economy to a new phase of growth. Under the Ford system, there is a clear division of labour between the brain and the body, with very fine division of tasks. As a result, there was a drastic increase in labour productivity, making possible the large scale production of industrial products and mass consumption.

In the 1960s, the Japanese manufacturing industry led by Toyota, based on Japanese cultural tradition and enterprise characteristics, underwent organic fusion with the Ford system and the flexible mode of production, creating the Toyota production mode, and motivating the modernisation of the Japanese industry and the overseas expansion of enterprises. Under the Toyota system, labourers are the long-term asset of enterprises, and the designers and producers could have interchanges without barriers, making possible the optimisation of the production scale based on the market situation.

Under the Ford system and the Toyota system, although many products have a multi-nodal value chain, yet enterprises compete on the total value chain. As the individual value nodes have not yet developed into independent industrial departments, a single value node will not have a significant impact on the result of the competition. Hence the two models are represented by the car industry. Before the 1990s, "Blue Giant" IBM and its competitors in Japan and Western Europe also followed the Ford system (some also encompassing the Toyota system), and the production system included hardware, software, after sales service and vertical systems such as financing and rentals.

Since the birth of the personal computer in the 1970s, the computer industry had a basis of horizontal division of labour that differs from that of the Ford system. With the software-hardware integration of Microsoft Windows and the Intel chip, the entire computer industry quickly shifted from a vertical structure to a horizontal structure. In the latter half of the 20th century, especially after the late 1980s, a new international production mode gradually formed, under Wintelism that had standards as the core. This took place against the background of the abandonment, crossing and breaking in between Ford and Toyota modes. This became a production mode that adapts to the international competition in the age of economic globalism under the conditions of high technology.

The characteristic of Wintelism is that it works around product standards against the background of effective global allocation of resources, resulting in the production and integration of product modules under the control of systems. In the entire process of completing the product value chain, the standard setters in the division of labour together with the module producer achieve a control mode based on win-win situation. Under Wintelism, the global production network uses multinational corporations as the vehicle and the horizontal mode or horizontal-vertical mode in the global value chain. In an industry based on division of labour according to production phases, there is the manifestation of drastic expansion of trade within the product, and this drives the depth and breadth of economic globalisation on a large scale.

Modularisation, outsourcing and mass customisation are the three supreme tools in enterprise operation under Wintelism. In contrast with Fordism that only pursues scale effect and scope effect, the agglomerative effect has an important role to play in "separation and integration" on the platform of Wintelism. It is actually with modularised production, outsourcing and supply chain management and the development of the modern logistics industry that Wintelistic enterprises can achieve mass production of new products within a short period of time.

Under Wintelism, speed is king. The focus of market competition is that while it maintains product differentiation, it also guarantees the speed of high-tech product introduction and industry upgrade, so as to achieve perfect intergration of constant product innovation and mass production. This drastically shortens the life cycle of traditional products. Once a new product is launched in the market, it will need to depend on the multinational production system to quickly complete the expansion of the global market. If a product is not expanded to other markets by the early stages of the product life cycle, the enterprise will have difficulty achieving economy of scale, and even achieving breakeven of the research and development costs.

To achieve the highest efficiency of production, accompanying the expansion of the global production network, the global FDI maintains its growth with a drastic increase in the number of multinational transactions in spare parts and semi-finished products. Since the 1990s, some developed countries have been shifting their capital-technology-intensive industries to developing countries, even including the higher value-added processes in their high-tech product production, such as research and development, processing manufacturing and services. This forms a new type of outsourcing and processing. Under this pattern, while the output countries (mainly developed countries) optimise their costs, the input countries (mainly newly industrialised economies and developing countries) will enhance their level of technology and optimise their industrial structure, thus achieving a win-win situation (See Figure 2. 2).

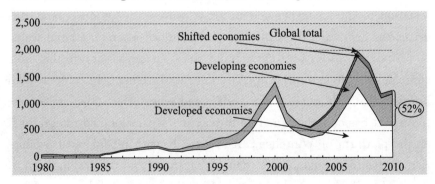

Figure 2. 2   Developing economies and shifted economies account for over half of the global FDI inflows (US$ billion)

Source: UNCTAD, *World Investment Report 2011*, p. 3.

If we say that the Ford system is a product of internalisation, and the Toyota mode is a product of industrialisation, then Wintelism is the inevitable result of economic globalisation. This new type of multinational production system reorganises the global industrial structure, and sharpens the sensitivity to scale and cost, bringing new opportunities and challenges to East Asia. In the production network of the East Asian region, the horizontal division of labour and trade have broken through the traditional "flying geese" mode and achieved rapid development. Since the mid 1990s, China has fast become the base of original equipment manufacturing (OEM). The huge market, low costs and the large pool of talent and supporting capacities have made China the top choice in the new round of global industrial transition.

Purchasing in China has become an irreplaceable component in the global production chain. China's cheap labour costs and the ability to achieve the required standard have benefitted a large number of multinational corporations. These companies look at their supply chain built up in China as an indispensable part of their global strategy. No internationally renowned high-tech company can complete their design, purchasing, production and sales without involving the Chinese market.

China captures capital, technology, machine and equipment from Japan, Korea and Taiwan of China, and imports high end spare parts and modular spare parts. China also imports resource products as well as primary and intermediary products from Southeast Asian countries, and at the same time acquires financial, legal and trade services from Singapore and Hong Kong of China. After processing, assembling, manufacturing and packaging, China exports the products to North America and European countries, or uses these products to satisfy domestic demands.

At the start of China's reform and opening-up in 1978, China's exports were ranked 32 globally. The introduction of the global value chain and the integration with the global and Southeast Asian production networks enabled China to achieve exports of US $ 62. 09 billion, US $ 249. 2 billion and US $ 1,201. 6 billion respectively in 1990, 2000 and 2009, and achieve global ranks of 15th, 7th and 1st position. Since

2002, and with the exception of 2009 due to the impact of the international financial crisis, China has maintained export growth rates of between 20% and 30%. Export demand has been one of the important pulling forces in the rapid development of the China economy for many years.

Relying on the strong brand effect and the global setting of the sales and service networks, developed countries have reaped the largest share of the profit in the global industrial value chain. On the other hand, China finds itself in the lower value adding parts of the production process, and reaps only the benefits of processing and assembly. Although the developed countries such as US and Europe have a deficit in their current account, yet their own industrial structure determines that the deficit will not reduce their employment rate, but actually increase their employment rate in the areas of research and development, sea transport, sales and marketing and financing. Correspondingly the manufacturing industries in developed countries have, to different extents, experienced the trend of "hollowing out".

From this, we can see that driven by market forces, China has assumed the position of a packaging and assembling centre in the global production network. Through the trade investment network, China and other economies have formed competitive and cooperative relationships in the industry chain or certain parts of the production line. This has formed a balance in the context of imbalance, and a win-win situation between the setters and implementers of standards and regulations.

At present, China has in reality become the world's product processing centre, one of the world's largest product suppliers, and one of the world's largest importers and exporters of goods and services. As the market vehicle for the mutual dependence of the Chinese economy and the global economy, the global production network will still achieve the bi-directional Magnet Effect. The Chinese economy cannot be separated from the world, and the global economy needs China. In short, China's development has become an organic part of global economic development.

"Long Planks" and "Short Planks" in the Global Market

Large Scale at Low Cost: China's Lore Tips

As one of China's fundamental state policy, the Reform and Opening-up Policy requires China to actively open up, fully enter the international market, take part in international division of labour, comply with international trade practices, and appropriately open up its boundaries—on the foundation of self-dependence and mutual benefit on fair grounds. The objective of this is to enable the inflow of essential elements from within and outside the country, the bi-directional flow of economic output, and the enhanced coupling and intergration of domestic and international markets, thus promoting China's economic development. With this as the starting point, and with the deepening of the degree of integration and the continued strengthening of the impact that the external environment has on the Chinese economy, the development of the Chinese economy will be a process that involves the constant integration of the global economy.

The added value that an economy acquires in the division of labour is determined by its position in the division of labour, and this in turn is determined by its essential resources. In general, economies with an abundance of technical resources will focus on research and development as well as equipment, and economies with an abundance of capital resources will focus on marketing. Economies with an abundance of labour resources mostly carry out processing, while they are relatively weak in scientific research and brand operations. In international trade, processing accounts for a relatively large proportion, "with two heads outside" and "with big input and big output" —China belongs to this category.

Under the principle of "of two evils choose the less", China has been riding on its strength of labour abundance and low costs in the international division of labour. In compliance with its commitments made at its entry into the WTO, China has perfected its policies on foreign capital industries, strengthened its protection of intellectual property, optimised its foreign investment environment, and realised the integration of foreign capital, technology and domestic labour resources, to achieve the development of its own economy and a win-win situation.

There is a Chinese saying "Make good use of local resources". Given China's geographic environment and its natural endowment of resources, China's economy and other economies in the world have different but complementary industry structures. The domestic industry structure determines the country's trade structure. In the meantime, differences in the endowment of resources, labour, technology, market, land and environment provide the basic conditions for the complementary trade activities between China and the world.

Although China is richly endowed, and most of the resources are self sufficient, there are two resources that are lacking—petroleum and iron ore. On top of these, there is also a shortage of timber and paper. On the other hand, these are inexhaustible resources in Southeast Asia, Africa, Australia and the Middle East. Take Russia as an example, the resources of China and Russia are very much complementary. China lacks natural resources and crude oil, while Russia lacks human resources and small commodities. Hence both are huge markets that complement each other.

China has to sell 800 million jeans to exchange an Airbus 380 plane. As China's top export market, top source of technology and second largest import market, the European Union and China complement each other in their economies. When "Designed in Europe" meets "Made in China", or when "European Technology" meets "Chinese Market", there is huge synergy.

Over a long period, China and the US have complemented each other in trade. "Made in China" and "Made in USA" have rarely been in direct competition. As the world factory, China needs the US market all the more, and the Chinese don't want to see the Americans living a frugal life or cut down on their shopping. The well developed virtual economy of the US needs back-up from China's robust manufacturing industry, and this is a truly win-win situation. Not only this, China's huge demand for disposable chopsticks, toothpicks and babies' diapers have be-

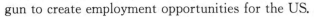
gun to create employment opportunities for the US.

The small and medium enterprises in China and in Japan are highly complementary. The former possesses an abundance of quality labour, while the latter has the advantage of higher technological content, stricter management, and an earlier entry into the international market. So trade, technology and investment are important areas for cooperation. One of the typical areas of China-Japan complementary trade is food trade. One quarter of China's export of food enters the Japanese market, and on the Japanese dining table, 90% of the garlic, peanuts and mushrooms come from China.

China also enjoys good complementary relationships with developing countries at similar development stages. This mostly takes the form of intra-industry trade that promotes each other's economic development. For instance, China and Malaysia and Thailand are complementary in the area of office machines, electrical appliances, and automatic data processing equipment. Meanwhile, China is complementary with Indonesia and the Philippines in the areas of iron and steel, machines and transport equipment. In the realm of textiles and garment, while China competes with ASEAN countries, they are also complementary in certain areas. First, China is a major producer of cotton, providing 70% of the raw materials of cotton fabric required by ASEAN countries. Second, ASEAN countries lack the capacity to renew their technical equipment, and China has textiles machinery for export. Third, there are different focuses in the raw materials and designs of their garment products, and there is room for complementary supplies in their export product structure.

The theory that different products and technologies have different product life cycles has inspired the Chinese who are wise and diligent. They know that the wheel of fortune favours different people at different times. With the continued reception of international industry transfer, and the production of mature products passed from other countries, China has time and again set world records for the number of years of high speed economic growth. Exercising both legs of technical import and autonomous research and development, China has firmly built its robust foundation of "low cost innovation and mass production". In competing and cooperating with world giants, Chinese enterprises have let no opportunities slip in enhancing their own competitiveness.

If we say that finding common grounds and living with differences is part of Chinese political wisdom, then the pursuit of complementary relationships, acting in harmony of the trends, and finding differences in common grounds is China's winning formula in the international division of labour.

Low Profit, High Quota: "Market Rule" Made in China

All the iPads in the hands of Apple fans are made in China. 2/3 of them were made in Chengdu, Sichuan or Chongqing, and the other 1/3 in Dongguan, Guangdong. Apart from pursuing synergy, scale economy is another lore tips for the Chinese economy. Indeed, as the traditional competitive edge is fading, scale economy is assuming greater and greater importance. What is different is that China's returns to scale is not manifested as greater excess profit, but as the ability to make the prices even lower, realising the maximisation of market share by keeping the profit margin narrow.

All the enterprises in the world would pursue maximum profit. This is in line with classical economics theories and people's common sense. However, what the Chinese industry did was to use minimal profit or even zero profit to compete for the largest share of the global market. Hence comes the saying "What is up when it is bought by China, what is down when it is sold by China".

So there are now two sayings: One of them is "never teach the Chinese to produce anything". And the other is "once the Chinese are producing, never produce the same thing". To take the US shoe industry as an example: for every 100 pairs of shoes the US imports, 97 are from China. The reason why there was not an incident similar to the "Shoes Burning Incident" in Elche City of Spain in September 2004 was because the shoe making workers in the US turned to selling shoes. In effect, the US shoe making industry has died by euthanasia.

When countries with innovative technologies like Japan and the US brought TV sets, video recorders, DVDs and cars to Chinese soil (measuring 9.6 million square kilometres), the products were already mature in their life cycle, and there was no need for the Chinese workers to repair. The market demand had already been developed through imports, and did not require Chinese enterprises to nurture it. China uses cost and scale as its weapon to create a production curve that is rising steeply. The ultimate purpose is not to acquire profit, but to achieve market share.

China does not have the high technology to form a global industry. China's natural resources compared to its enormous population size is not particularly rich. China's financial development is not advanced. The Chinese people are not particularly noted for their labour productivity. However, despite the "good for nothing" impression that people have, China has won the market and stunned the world, and achieved the goal of "bringing a heavy fist out of a light one". This is indeed China's only advantage.

According to the *Financial Times* of UK, in 2010, China has already occupied 19.8% of the world's manufacturing output, slightly higher than the 19.4% of the US, and has become the country with the highest manufacturing output in the world, displacing the US from this enviable position that it had occupied for over 110 years. Economic historians believe that in 1830, China's manufacturing output nearly reached 30% of the global output. In 1900 it dwindled to about 6%, and in 1990 it further shrank to about 3%. From that time on, China has been fast chasing after the US, riding on its lower labour costs and formidable foreign investments.

In recent years, of the 15 billion pairs of shoes produced worldwide, "Made in China" already exceeded 10 billion pairs, or 67% of the total, making China the world's largest shoe making base and shoe exporting country. According to the data released by market survey company Display Search in November 2011, in the first nine months of 2011, the 10 top producers of LCD TV sets included three Chinese enterprises—TCL, Hisense and Skyworth. Meanwhile, Changhong and Konka are also high on the sales chart. At present, Chinese enterprises already account for over 20% of the global LCD TV market, posing a real threat to Japan and Korea, which account for 36% and 30% of the global market respectively. While China commands the domestic market, Chinese enterprises are setting their sight on the overseas market. A decade after China's entry into the WTO, Chinese textile and garment products have acquired 1/3 of the global market share. However, it is still in a difficult situation where trade disputes take place.

The internationally renowned company Huawei is expanding its successful practice from the telecom equipment market to other markets. The practice is to compete for market share by selling products at a low price. In 2011, Huawei's sold 20 million smart phones—a 500% increase over the previous year. In 2012, this figure is expected to double. The cheaper smart phones asserted pressure on Taiwan enterprises such as HTC. Now also in the network equipment market, Huawei is still named by Cisco CEO John Chambers as Cisco's most powerful competitor.

At present, foreign capital is gradually shifting to the open arms of Southeast Asian economies, although they are inferior to China in terms of infrastructure, auxiliary production systems, consumption demands, as well as legal and financial systems. This is due to the rising costs of labour, land and environment in China. Starting from autumn and winter of 2012, consumers will see that some of the shirts on sale at VANCL are not "Made in China", but "Made in Bangladesh". In the last analysis, "Made in China" at first used cheap labour as its competitive advantage. Then it thrived on returns of scale and comprehensive support. If we say that Wall Street in the US made use of their highly developed financial system to build the best virtual economy, then against the background of China's special circumstances, "Made in China" at least built the best real economy in terms of expanding its market share.

Although in the words of Alan Tonelson—a researcher at the conservative US research institution of US Business and Industry Council—China's displacement of the US as the world's largest manufacturing country was a "wake-up call", yet the US still commands a big productivity advantage. In 2010, the US was slightly behind China in terms of manufacturing output, yet the US manufacturing industry employed only 11. 5 million workers while China employed 150 million. Moreover, in China's manufacturing output, a large percentage comes from subsidiary companies of US enterprises, using US technology. This is particularly evident in the electronics industry.

The path of "low profit, high market share" is not sustainable. On the one hand, China needs to have a good understanding of international division of labour, and learn the art of win-win, multiple wins, and all win. On the other hand, "Made in China" needs to enhance its quality and carry out transformation and upgrading. In the life cycle of a product, the acquisition of high technology does not necessarily entail higher prices or higher profit. In fact, high technology sometimes can give our industry another competitive weapon—low cost under high efficiency. Low costs plus high technology will become China's supreme weapon after the upgrading of the Chinese industries (See Figure 2. 3).

Figure 2. 3   "Made in China" has conquered the world,
and looks forward to changes in quality

"Change" or "No Change" on the Global Economic Pattern

Cooperation in Competition or Competition in Cooperation?

In the age of economic globalisation, to pursue their own economic development, each of the economies puts interest as the starting point for handling international economic relationships. If we say that the basis of international politics is hegemony, then the basis of global economy is interest. Driven by interest, between alliance and cruel competition, there is usually a narrow margin. Competition promotes human improvement, and an alliance can reap huge benefits brought by scale and synergy. Hence, cooperation and competition are in real existence, driven by market forces in the process of globalisation.

Whether it is between developed economies, or between developed economies and developing economies, or among developing economies, cooperation and competition coexist in trade. Moreover, cooperation will promote greater depth and expansion, and competition will promote greater diversity and intensity. For cooperation between developed economies and developing economies to materialise, the reason is that the former puts more emphasis on gaining permission to enter the market, and the latter further hopes to acquire advanced technology and management experience. The existence of competition between developing economies is because they have fewer differences in terms of economic structure, endowment of essential elements, level of demand, and science and technology. In the meantime, there are fewer complementary relations and weaker asymmetry in complementary and mutual reliance. As a result, conflict and competition often coexist in the introduction of foreign capital, the fight for foreign assistance, import and the fight for export markets.

International trade is the direct manifestation of economic competition. On the one hand, it created imbalance in the global economy; on the other hand, it is also a preliminary form of economic cooperation. It ensures the interflow of tangible and intangible goods between different economies. It is also the effective allocation of resources and the re-distribution of wealth.

Under Wintelism, the global production network is a medium-view platform for competition and cooperation. It ensures that competition takes place in a benevolent direction that ultimately becomes cooperation that achieves sustainable development. The "invisible hand" of the market works through the global production network, and in a bottom-up mode drives the development of competition and cooperation among economies, forming the "competition-cooperation" mode in the context of global economic relationships.

The Preferential Trade Agreements (PTAs) —either regional or multi-regional—and the WTO are the macro platform for "competition and cooperation" (See Table 2. 1). In response to the fierce competition under the conditions of economic globalisation, various economies are promoting unification of regional economies as a strategic tool for achieving competitive advantage. In today's world, there are three major regional cooperation modules—the European Union (EU), the North America Free Trade Area (NAFTA), and the Asia-Pacific Economic Cooperation (APEC), CAFTA, and the ASEAN 10+3 Conference.

Table 2. 1   Overview of Effective PTAs in the World in 2012

(Either on Record or Not on Record)

	Bilateral	Multi-lateral	Multi-lateral; at lease one party is PTA
Between developed countries	6	9	8
Between developed and developing countries	29	6	41
Between developing countries	135	36	18
Intra-regional	81	39	26
Inter-regional	89	12	41

Source: WTO Secretariat, *World Trade Report 2011*, p. 61.

Since the 21st century, China has been playing a pivotal role in global import-export trade. It has become the biggest trade partner for a number of economies, and a hub for processing and manufacturing in the global production network. China practises an integrated strategy for economic and trade cooperation, coordinating global interests with the interests of regional entities. Indeed, China is taking part in international economic cooperation in a larger scope, at a higher level, and to a greater depth.

On the one hand, China is actively taking part in multi-lateral trade agreements. It made a constructive impact in the Doha round of talks in the WTO, submitted over 100 propositions, and entered the core of the talks, in order to promote an international trade environment that is more open and fair. On the other hand, China also attaches much importance to launching bilateral and regional trade cooperation. It has accumulatively set up 163 bilateral trade cooperation mechanisms, signed 129 bilateral investment agreements, and gradually become the architect of regional economic unification. China has signed 10 FTAs with developed and developing countries such as New Zealand, Singapore, Chile and Peru, and 6 more FTAs are under negotiation. In 2010, the ASEAN-China Free Trade Area (ACFTA) was officially launched, and became the largest FTA among developing countries, actively driving the process of economic unification in East Asia. Up to the end of 2010, China has 14 FTAs under negotiation, involving 31 countries or territories, with bilateral trade amounting to US $ 521.3 billion, accounting for 25% of China's total foreign trade volume.

As strengthened dialogue and deeper cooperation become the major theme in the handling of economic affairs in different countries, the real and potential competition among various economies has always existed. For instance, in the area of new energy (such as clean energy), China-US cooperation has entered a substantive stage, and in the competition for global new energy sources, the two countries are strong and direct competitors. In October 2010, the Office of the United States Trade Representative, in accordance with Clause 301 of the US Trade Act of 1974, carried out investigation into the complaint of the US steel workers against China for using new energy sources such as domestic wind and solar energy to implement protective policies, thereby providing "unfair assistance". So the China-US competition for new energy has finally moved from the back stage to the front stage.

In various forms of competition and cooperation, it is possible to form among various economies a macro and micro level of benevolent interaction, to drive the formation of an active and spiraling trend in competition and cooperation, thereby generating a positive effect. The static effect of competition and cooperation comes mainly from cooperation, including economic growth, expansion of trade investment, and the rise in welfare level. The dynamic effect mainly comes from competition, including the upgrade of industry structure, enhancement of competitive advantage, and the strengthening of external competitiveness. Under the checks and balances of market rules, the manifestations of competition and cooperation form a mutually beneficial, all-win situation.

The most militant form of economic competition among economies is trade friction. In the first decade of the 21st century, the aggravation of international trade protectionism is caused by the imbalance in the development of various economies, the competitiveness in industry and trade structure, the exclusivity in the regional trade groups, the contradictions in the allocation of trade benefits, and the politicisation of trade issues. The various economies have used various "weapons" to save their trades and to strengthen the protection of their domestic industries and markets.

We can say that as globalisation has developed to the status today, there has been increasing interdependence among the different economies. It is practically impossible to return to the times when the economies operated in isolation, treating each other as enemies. Today, trade protectionism is manifested as: under the banner of fair trade, there is the full practice of anti-dumping, countervailing and special safeguard measures. The technical barriers, such as product quality standards, technical capability standards, health inspection and quarantine standards, have become new means of trade protectionism. In addition, trade friction has increasingly created repercussions in more of the economic and social realms. Emission reduction standards, social security and foreign exchange systems have become causes of friction.

With Chinese exports sweeping the international market, tangible and intangible trade barriers against China's traditional export goods and some high-tech products have appeared in one form or another. According to WTO figures, China has for the past 17 years been the biggest target for anti-dumping and countervailing complaints among WTO members. In fact, 35% of the world's anti-dumping and 71% of the world's countervailing complaints involve China.

Since 2010, the European and US debt crises have been causing instability and imbalance in the process of recovery for the global economy. Against this background, China has become a region of heavy disaster in international trade protectionism. On the one hand, China exercises its rights as a member of the WTO, determined to protect its national interests and industry interests, and to respond well to trade frictions. On the other hand, it has taken solid measures against trade protectionism. During the spread of the international financial crisis in 2008, China organised over 30 procurement delegations overseas, to promote the growth of imports and foreign investments.

In 2010, Chinese export goods have become the target of 66 cases of investigation into trade remedy, involving an amount up to US$7.14 billion. In 2011, the Spanish government introduced a policy regulation to counter the import of shoes. It made a comparison on shoes of similar style and material—between imported shoes and shoes in the customs catalogue. If the declared price of a certain batch of shoes is lower than the prices listed in the customs catalogue, the goods will be impounded. It is only when the tariffs, value-added taxes and fines are paid on the shoes that the goods can be retrieved. Meanwhile, 40 large enterprises in the US implemented on 1 December 2011 a new industry standard, limiting the lead content of products such as handbags and shoes. The coverage of this new standard is likely to be extended to waist belts and other ornaments.

Since 2012, trade protection measures targeted against China have grown dramatically. In the first three months, the number grew by 80%, mainly in the areas of new energy, iron and steel, industrial chemicals, textiles, and intellectual property. The European Union has even made subtle suggestion that they will initiate anti-dumping and countervailing investigations into China's photovoltaic and wireless products. German enterprise Solar World has lodged a complaint to the European Commission demanding an anti-dumping investigation against China's photovoltaic products. If the anti-dumpling and countervailing investigation against the wireless products of Huawei and ZTC eventually goes ahead, it may become the biggest of such investigations in terms of the money involved.

The US has been constantly criticising the RMB exchange rate mechanism and China's trade policy. However, the fact is that the US is the biggest beneficiary in the China-US trade relationship. On the one hand, it demands that China protect its intellectual property, and on the other hand, it imposes lots of restrictions against China's importing of high technology. On the one hand, it demands all sorts of preferential treatment in its investments in China; on the other hand, it sets up all sorts of barriers against China's investing in the US. These are all in contravention of the principles of win-win international trades, fairness, and synergy.

"Self Enjoyment" or "Enjoyment For All"?

There is a saying in Confucian philosophy that "Self enjoyment is not as good as enjoyment for all. " This has inspired the creation of a new term in the context of global economy: inclusive growth. Indeed this has become a mega trend in global economy (See Figure 2. 4). The world "inclusive" originally means "extensively embracing and compatible". The concept of "inclusive growth" was first raised by the Asian Development Bank in 2007, and was progressively perfected by various international economic organisations. Basically it means embracing all, and beneficial to all parties. It also means non-acceptance of one party enjoying all the benefits.

Figure 2. 4   "Inclusive growth" is the coordinated economic, social and environmental development among different stakeholder communities

Inclusive growth means letting more people enjoy the fruit of globalisation, protecting the underprivileged communities, and maintaining a balance between man and nature in the pursuit of economic growth. Inclusive growth advocates a mode of development that is more comprehensive and balanced, and that overcomes the shortcomings of single-minded economic growth. The idea is to put economic growth on a sustainable parallel path with social progress, livelihood improvement and the protection of resources and environment.

First of all, there are a change in the pattern of global resource allocation, and a trend towards balance in global economic forces. More and more newly industrialised countries have joined the global allocation of production and capital. Brazil, Russia, India, China, and South Africa (BRICS — "gold brick countries") are becoming important driving forces in global economic growth.

As for the newly industrialised countries today, their growth rates in most cases are higher than that of developed economies. Their rapid development has effectively hedged the economic recession on other markets. Hence they are enjoying an increasing right of word and the right to set prices in the development of the global economy, and playing an indispensable role in the global allocation of resources. From 2001 to 2010, the economic growth rate for newly industrialised economies averaged over 6%, far higher than the average for developed countries of 2.6% and the global average of 4.1%. In 2010, the GDP of China, India and Brazil grew by 10.3%, 9.7% and 7.5% respectively.

The BRICS countries are exercising an increasing influence on the global market. In the global commodities market, China's demand for petroleum, metal ore and soya beans, Russia's supply of petroleum and natural gas, Brazil's supply of iron ore and coffee are all major supply-demand forces in the global market, capable of influencing the market prices in the global commodities market. In the international financial market, the BRICS countries possess large quantities of overseas assets. Hence, changes in the allocation of their overseas assets and changes in multi-national capital flow will have great impact on the exchange rates and interest rates of major currencies in the world.

Meanwhile, the business modes of newly industrialised market economies are also undergoing change. Scale economy plus innovative high technology have become the general choice of newly industrialised economies. They are all striving to realise the intensification of production, develop new energy sources, conserve energy, and develop electronic information and biotechnology. They are driving the optimisation of structure and upgrading of industry, in order to set up modernised production systems that match their own resource endowments. In addition, the Chiang Mai Initiative with a scale of US $ 120 billion has set up a multi-lateral mechanism and the Asian debt market has set up internal markets. All these have contributed to the scenario of active growth for these newly industrialised economies.

From the point of view of the characteristics of the global production network, we can see that with the modularization and integration being the basic thinking of modern industrial production, the pattern of international production changed. The trend is for the value chain to be diversified, with the development of sharing activities. The separation and integration of the different nodes of the industry value chain has become the norm for international trade.

China has become the hub for processing, assembling and manufacturing in the East Asian production network. On the one hand, China can put the various economies, each at a different stage, into the same modern international production system, so that all the participants can ride on their own specific advantage to benefit from the huge welfare of economic globalisation. On the other hand, China, as an active participant in the international flow of global commodities and fundamentals, is changing from its export-oriented development strategy to a strategy that pays equal attention to imports and exports, and promotes trade balance. In China's import demands, the "indirect demand" such as the spare parts and intermediate products used for export to US and European markets is commanding a smaller and smaller percentage, whereas the "direct demand" for products used to satisfy China's own consumers is commanding a larger and larger share.

The flow and source of the global FDI is another perspective for observing the inclusivity of the global economy. Developing countries such as China, and the transitional economies, have year by year become an important supporting force for the global growth in FDI. The total absorbed foreign capital in 2010 has become comparable to the developed economies.

After the subprime crisis, the global financial centres of Wall Street and the City of London were hit hard, and their capability to allocate global resources was undermined. This provided a good opportunity for China to allocate global resources to suit its own interest. This is real "going out". In the process of integrating global funds and technologies, China is gradually shifting from being the "world factory" to becoming the "world investor", and from successor to creator. China is also shifting from the "receiver" role to the role of "maker". Towards the end of the 12th Five-year Plan, with "economy for the Chinese" (manifested as GNP) chasing behind "Chinese economy" (manifested as GDP), China can hope to see a balance in import and export. This will be an important step for China to grow from being a "big country" to being a "strong country".

Then there are changes to the global production pattern. Global economic growth shifted from a mode that relies on virtual demand growth to one that relies on real demand growth. High oil prices have made the original global production-sale mode shift to an adjustment more tuned to inclusive growth.

On the one hand, since the subprime crisis, market forces started to carry out adjustments on the mode of resource allocation in the virtual economy characterised by excessively high returns. The developed countries also started to make adjustments in the direction of resurrecting the manufacturing industry.

Gordon Brown, the British Prime Minister, was the first to propose that UK must resurrect its manufacturing industry. Subsequently US President Barack Hussein Obama Ⅱ stressed that in 2015, the United States' exports need to double and 2 million jobs need to be created. At the end of 2009, Buffett acquired BNSF Railway and people were led to believe that the company should have good prospects that captured the guru's attention. Then the European Union stressed in 27 countries the importance of developing the manufacturing industry. Then Japan also stressed the urgency of resurrecting the manufacturing industry. When newly industrialised economies tend to use domestic market demand to drive the recovery of the manufacturing industry, the growth towards newly emerging markets becomes an essential factor that pulls developed countries towards the recovery of their manufacturing industry.

On the other hand, the sustainable high level of international oil prices has caused the global transport costs to soar. This creates a lot of uncertainty in the pattern of allocation of fundamentals in global markets, and in the determination of the price of the fundamentals. It also impacts on the modes of global production and sales.

To save transport costs, a lot of multinational corporations are abandoning their globalised mode of production and sales, and calls back their production lines and assembly lines to their own country or neighbouring regions. A lot of US electronics manufacturers are moving their production lines from China to Mexico, which is much closer, and the US consumers found that there are more and more products that are "Made in USA". In 2009, Nike closed down its only shoe factory in China—the Taicang Factory, and Adidas China's headquarters will also close down in 2012 their only direct subsidiary factory in Suzhou. Leading shoe manufacturers Clarks, K-Swiss and Bakers are also building additional plants in Vietnam and Indonesia. With more foreign capital moving from China to Southeast Asian countries with cheaper fundamentals, the goods on the shelves of US supermarkets are no longer just Chinese goods, but goods from many other countries. Diversification has set in.

Second, the international currency system has become more diversified and competitive. The system is on its path of multi-polarisation in the global gaming, while the expedition of RMB regionalisation and internationalisation has aroused extensive concern in the international community.

First, the US Dollar is still at the core of global currency exchange reserves, international payment and clearing. However, its hegemonious status has been undercut. Various other countries have set up diversified reserve pools, and the demand for the use of original currency for clearing in trading is a new trial on the adjustment of a single currency system.

Second, the Euro, as a trendsetting product of European unification, is facing serious challenges. Yet the political desire for Europe to be united still persists. As long as Germany, France and Italy have no intention to eliminate it, the Euro Zone will continue to exist.

Third, China has, in the past decade or so, maintained a double surplus in its international income and expenditure. This has progressively raised the RMB's international competitiveness and influence. With the perfection of the financial market and regulatory system, the RMB's capital projects will progressively be opened up. In 2006, the RMB's liquidity in the international market exceeded that of the Japanese Yen. In ASEAN countries and Hong Kong, Macau and Taiwan of China, the volume of flow and the volume of deposits have both seen improvements. Following Nigeria's and Thailand's announcement about accepting the RMB into their financial reserves in September and November 2011, Saudi Arabia in May 2012 also accepted the RMB into their reserves, to further realise foreign exchange diversification. In July 2012, the central bank of Indonesia started to buy RMB issued by China to price the securities, and also accepted RMB assets into its foreign currency reserves. It is estimated that the RMB contained in the world's foreign currency reserves amounted to about US $ 15 billion to US $ 20 billion.

Finally, the international cooperation that drives the response to climate changes has achieved some progress, and China has made significant contributions. In recent years, China has become the largest country to implement measures to save energy and reduce emissions, and to compensate for environmental deficits.

In December 1997, the "United Nations Framework Convention on Climate Change " was convened in Osaka, Japan. In the third meeting the parties passed the "Kyoto Protocol", which aims to limit the emission of greenhouse gases by developed countries. The Kyoto Protocol stipulates that by 2010, the emission of six greenhouse gases, such as carbon dioxide, must be reduced by 5. 2% compared with 1990. The US refused to accept this agreement, thinking that it would hinder its economic growth. They even complained that the Kyoto Protocol did not include countries like China and India, and did not require them to reduce their emissions. In April 2001 and in December 2011, the US and

Canada withdrew from the Kyoto Protocol. Meanwhile, Japan and Russia adopted a rather passive attitude. As a result, the leadership of the European Union in managing global climate change had weakened.

Objectively speaking, the developed countries that have "luxury emissions" are willing to shoulder some responsibilities. However, as they are worried that newly industrialised nations and the developing countries may not be able to cooperate, the plan fell through. "Survival emission" countries that are newly industrialised are worried that emission reduction would hinder their industrialization process. Meanwhile, what the developing countries are most worried about is the capital for emissions reduction, source of technology, and whether they are able to enable the newly industrialised and developing countries to benefit from the emission reduction through the new emissions reduction pledges. Hence without cooperation by the south and the north, there would be no hope. If we do not "contain" the considerations, there would be no hope for emissions reduction.

From the Cobanhagan Conference of 2009 to the Cancun Conference in 2010 and then to the Durban Conference in 2011, international climatic cooperation had not yet gained any real progress. But what we can see is, the demands of the newly emerging market economies have been expressed more fully. Based on the pattern of industries and the global production, developing countries like China are, in the global industry chain, occupying positions characterised by processing and assembling, low value added, and high carbon emission. Yet their products mostly end up in developed countries. The principle that "Consumer pays" is a relatively fair and reasonable emission reduction principle. Regarding the carbon emission in the process of production, it is possible to levy a tax based on the stage of final consumption. The greening of the production process and the greening of the consumption process are both indispensable. In the global green movement, China has always insisted on the "common but distinct responsibility" principle, manifesting the image of a great responsible country with sincerity, determination and confidence.

"Multi-polarisation" or "Non-polarisation"?

Economic globalisation suggests that a "unified market" in the global context is gradually forming. This means that the economic activities of various economies are intertwined—there is me in you, and there is you in me. This also suggests that a set of "market game rules" is being formed globally. This is tantamount to the setting up of general rules and common mechanism for regulating economic behaviours in the global context.

Under these conditions and environment, interests formed by a unified market and unified game rules are being allocated globally. While economic globalisation enables participants to reap a profit, yet the balance of interests is definitely not balanced. The fact that developed countries are controlling the global economic authorities will not be changed in the short term. The importance of developing countries in the global economy is still inferior to developed countries, and developing countries are still not in a good position to steer the development of the global economy. There is not yet a dramatic change in relative strength between the two camps in the global economy, and the process of the core of the global economy shifting to the Asia Pacific region will be very long.

From the perspective of the global distribution of demand, the world now has a population of about 7 billion, and China and India together embraces 2. 5 billion, with an annual consumption of US $ 6,000 billion. Among these, China has a population of 1. 3 billion, with an annual consumption of US $ 3,700 billion. On the other hand, the US has a population of 300 million, yet their annual consumption amounts to US $ 11,000 billion. Hence the US plays a pivotal role in the global economy. Under the condition of the global economy having an excess, a trade deficit is the manifestation of power. The US rides on its international credit status and provides consumption credit through the excessive issue of currency, to directly pay for import to maintain its status as the final realiser and absorber of products around the world.

From the standpoint of the world's new round of growth and innovation driving force, we can see that after the 2008 international financial crisis, the global economy is slowly recovering, but there is a lot of uncertainty. Although the needs and innovations that drive the next round of phenomenal growth in the global economy are still unclear, yet judging from who won the Nobel Price over the years, or from where there is a constant generation of applied science breakthroughs, we can perhaps deduce that the US will still be spearheading the next round of drastic development and innovation. Meanwhile, new energy sources may be the area where there will first be breakthroughs, and this may be the most promising direction.

Many achievements in the high-tech area in the 20th century—from semi-conductor materials in the 1950s, micro-computers in the 1970s, biotechnology in the 1980s to the IT industry in the 1990s—were all spearheaded by the US in completing the industrialisation of the innovative technology and the creation of huge economic benefits. The multi-level financial market in the US has provided to various kinds of investors a diversified range of escape routes, as well as the mechanism for the socialisation and internationalisation of risk. This enabled the US to gain the initiating right in individual division of labour, and the strategic command position in international competition.

Since the 21st century, the US has excelled in using innovation to enhance the added value of their products and services. The source of value is the intellect, and the vehicle for value is intangible products. There is extensive space for development for the value added that this innovation can carry, and the speed of this innovation is far greater than the enhancement of the production process of tangible products. In the meantime, the risk of intangible wastage and storage depreciation has been transferred to the newly emerging economies in East Asia, including China. The apps economy induced by companies like Facebook, Google and Apple is still prevalent in the US, and this industry has employed over 300,000 employees, and related games and virtual products have swept the market outside the US.

The pattern of benefit distribution—whether it is the core business of key technologies or the production of high end spare parts, or the global realisation of product standards, commercial regulations and final value—is still in the hands of major developed countries. They use standards to consolidate global resources, creating a pattern of global production, distribution and exchange. Developing countries like China are mainly engaged in the processing and assembling of products, and have not been able to gain the winning advantage in the key positions of the industry chain. Neither can they control the direction of flow of global essential resources and fundamentals.

In general, from raw materials to products, and then to the hands of the consumers, if the time required is 100%, then not more than 10% of the time is in the realm of production while the rest of the time is in the realm of circulation. The fact is that the developed countries are controlling the process of research and development, as well as the process of circulation, creating a huge chain of benefits. US business leader Walmart has for many years been at the top of the world's 500 top corporations, and this is food for thought. By 6 December 2011, Walmart has set up 358 shopping centres in 133 cities in 21 provinces in China. 80% of the shopping centres are in cities outside China's first-tier cities.

Although China has grown up, yet its attribute as a developing country has not changed. There is still a wide gap in world ranking between China's total GDP and its per capita average GDP. China's per capital economic capacity is still far behind developed countries—only a-bout 10% of the US and Japan, and is in about 120th position in world ranking. Even in the total economic volume, China is still below half of the US or the European Union, and the World Bank and IMF are still categorising China as a medium income country.

In terms of labour productivity index, autonomous innovation capacity and financial capability, there is also a wide gap between China and advanced countries. Charles Wolf Jr. , senior researcher at the Hoover Institution on War, Revolution and Peace at Stanford University, thinks that although the US is experiencing a decline in some significant indices, this is only a relative decline. In some areas that are hard to quantify, such as the factor of mechanisms that promote innovative spirit, and cultural, intellectual property and legal factors, the US still commands an advantage over other countries.

It took the US about 100 years to overtake UK as the world's top economy. It took Japan, rising from the ruins of the Second World War, 30 years to become the world's second largest economy. China's total economic volume can hope to overtake the US in 15 to 20 years. But although overtaking in terms of total GDP has a special significance, yet this does not equate to overtaking in terms of integrated national strength. Neither does it signify the end of the US-led international economic pattern or the global situation. Putting the clock forward in terms of China's total economic volume is only a matter of viewpoint on the political and economic forum that discusses topics like RMB exchange rate. We need to be clear about this (See Figure 2.5).

Figure 2.5   Betting companies are launching new products based on when the Chinese economy will overtake the US

Part 3

Model and Structure

"Every road leads to Rome." On the road to economic development, there is no single standard mode that applies to every situation.

Life is always changing and unpredictable. In the context of the ever-changing global economy, there is no successful model to replicate—only true cases to make reference to. Today's heaven may become tomorrow's hell. Today's success may even be tomorrow's curse.

In the face of the horrific waves of the global economy, the only thing we can do is to constantly adjust our direction, steer clear of the hidden reefs, and take on the wind and rain. It is only in this way that this gigantic ship called "Chinese economy" can ride on the wind and waves to reach the shore of success.

China cannot replicate the success of the developed countries. The China today is not the replica of the history of the developed countries. The model of economic growth of these developed countries will not be the road of development for the China of tomorrow. In particular the path of growth for the US today will never be the only path for China's economic development.

China's reform and opening-up has created a path that suits the future development of the Chinese economy. The rapid development of China for three decades or so has reaped abundant results. The total size of the Chinese economy has soared to No. 2 position globally—the rise of China is nothing less than a miracle.

With the rapid development of the Chinese economy, the conflicts and contradictions accumulated in the process of reform became more and more apparent. In the post-crisis era the uncertainty of the global economic situation means that China is likely to face greater and greater risks. The worries about economic model, the dilemma between fairness and efficiency, the surprises of the road of exploration, the pitfalls of the middle income group, and the way to clearly define China's positioning in the global economic system and to merge with the tides of economic globalisation—all of these require China to steer and paddle with dexterity, and constantly adjust its direction of sailing.

Is changing of growth model a means or an end in the context of China's economic development? Is it the process or the result? Is it dynamic or static? The Chinese mode needs to be constantly adjusted and innovated on the basis of developments in the world and within the country. It needs to be constantly perfected and developed in handling the changes.

Chinese Model: "Teething Problems"

Why "Other People's Today" Is Not "My Tomorrow"?

Following its reform and opening-up, China has created its own development mode in the tide of the global economy. Summing up the basic truths over the past three decades or so, we can crystallise them into the Chinese Economic Mode that has made unique achievements in the context of the global economy.

In the economics lectures at Chinese universities today, when it comes to the reasons for reform and opening-up, the stress is invariably on the contradictions between advanced production relationships and backward productivity. But if I tell you that when Deng Xiaoping advocated reform and opening-up, the Chinese people on one-third of the country's terrain were living a life that was worse than that in the 1930s, not too many people will believe me. But this is the bare truth!

If we take 60 years from 1949, when the People's Republic of China was established, to 2009, then these 60 years will encompass the 30 years before the reform and opening-up, and the 30 years after. If we calculate the added wealth in those 60 years—that is, adding up the GDP—then the figure would run to about RMB 250,000 billion. In the 30 years before the reform and opening-up, China generated only 2% of its wealth, while the remaining 98% was generated in the 30 years after the reform and opening-up policy was implemented. The last 8 years of these 60 years was when China was in the WTO, and these 8 years accounted for two-thirds of the newly acquired wealth. Hence we can say that the reform and opening-up policy had a huge impact on China's economic development.

30 years ago, nobody in China would have imagined that nearly everyone would own a mobile phone, and that a lot of people would be driving a car. Nobody would have imagined that out of every 35 persons one would be living in either Beijing or Shanghai, and that over 50% of the population would be living in cities or towns. This rapid development of cities and towns was almost without precedent in the world.

In the last century, Japan's two plans to double the income of the people turned the Japanese economy from the ruins of the Second World War to No. 2 position in the world. This stunned the world at that time. Today, China has also become one of the engines of global economic growth, and it also took 30 years—one generation—to complete this overwhelming change.

30 years ago, the Chinese would never have imagined that China would become the factory of the world in three decades. The competitiveness of "Made in China" products has created similar shockwaves around the world. This was not because China produced a lot of high-tech products with core competitiveness. Just the opposite—this was because while everybody thought China had not mastered the core technologies, they could not but admit that Chinese products were extremely competitive in the international market.

What puzzled the Chinese even more was that in these 30 years, China's GDP had been growing at an annual average of 9.8%. This growth rate changed China itself, and shocked the world. However, the whole world, including the Chinese themselves, suddenly exclaimed: "This mode cannot be sustained. China must reform!" This is really beyond comprehension.

In his visit to Australia, US President Obama clearly stated that China's over 1 billion people cannot live the life that Americans or Australians live, and if they really did, that would spell catastrophe for the earth. First of all, this highlights the unsustainability of the American Mode. China has realised that the present economic mode must be reformed. The question is: how to reform, and in what direction.

"Growth", "Development", or "Rise in Peace"?

If we explore the economic accomplishments of the People's Republic of China since its inception over 60 years ago from the standpoint of development economics, we will find some economists label this as "growth" while others would label it as "development", and still others would call it "rise in peace". In describing the economic development process, these three terms are related, but are also distinct from each other.

Today, when people evaluate the economic situation of a developed country, they generally use the word "growth" instead of "development". But when referring to a developing country, both words are used. But to describe a very special country, like China, they would use the term "rise". These differences highlight the natures of different modes of economic progress.

The Western academia, especially Western economists, are generally of the view that developed countries have a basically sound economic system, and their economic structure can autonomously and endogenously generate changes based on market demand. From the political perspective, the "tripartite" system with the legislature, administration and judiciary being the three pillars of society seems to be near perfect, and the entire political process is also nearing perfection. Also, the civic society of the Western world seems to be more harmonious. Hence people do not tend to think that this type of society would have qualitative change, or that there would be any dramatic changes to the system or structure. Then people tend to use the word "growth" to describe the economy of the developed countries, meaning that changes or expansion,

if any, would be purely quantitative, while qualitative changes or leaps would be inconceivable.

To describe developing countries, academics tend to use both "growth" and "development". This means that while there is quantitative growth, there is also qualitative developments in terms of economic and management system. The economic structure of developing countries is not perfect, and on the political front, the democratic system and civic society have not been totally put in place or kept healthy. Hence these developing countries will inevitably experience a process of transition with both quantitative and qualitative changes. And the quantitative economic changes will inevitably be the basis for subsequent qualitative changes. So when people mention developing countries, they will use these two terms at the same time.

As for "rise", it basically means a dramatic expansion in economic aggregate within a short period, and at the same time there are drastic and systemic changes in the economic life of the country. To be sure, the word "rise" has not been a positive term for many years. For example, during the Second World War, the word "rise" was used to describe the rise of the German empire. However, as people use the word to describe China's economic growth, they add the word "peace", making it "rise in peace", mainly to say that the Chinese economy has rapidly expanded over a short period, and there has been fundamental changes to the economic system and structure.

With this kind of rapid change, the entire social life in China was completely different from the past. At the same time there have been conflicts in the external environment, with increasing pressure. For a country to undergo such fundamental changes within such a short time, it would be difficult for people in China and people outside to adapt to these changes. But to realise sustainable economic growth, it would be necessary to reform the economic development mode.

Using "Internal Change" to Respond to "External Change"

The tide of the global economy is ever-changing and unpredictable. To explore and understand the mode of China's economic development and structural reforms, we must first understand the external economic environment for China's economic development, especially the changed global economy and the environmental constraints.

For a long time, people generally have recognised that the global economy is out of balance, and that this "imbalance" was formed in the process of economic globalisation. There is also the consensus that "After losing balance there is a need to regain the balance." However, with the development and evolution of the global economy, the meaning of "imbalance" and "balance" has undergone fundamental changes. The meaning of "world economic imbalance" changed from "imbalance between the rich and the poor" to "imbalance of the current account". In the meantime, the word "imbalance" in the realm of global economics is increasingly being used to mean the imbalance in the current account of international revenue and expenditure between developed countries and emerging market economy —or the unsustainability of current accounts. The trade deficits of developed countries and the trade surpluses of emerging market economies have caused the unsustainability of the global economy.

The "balance" between the rich and the poor is now of only secondary importance. What we need to "re-balance" is the surpluses and deficits of the recurrent account. The trade surplus of emerging market economies should be drastically reduced in order to help developed countries overcome their trade deficits. From the perspective of economic imbalance, China's economic development model that is still driven by external demand is under question. The Chinese economic development mode "borrowing east wind" that has helped suddenly changed direction (See Figure 3.1).

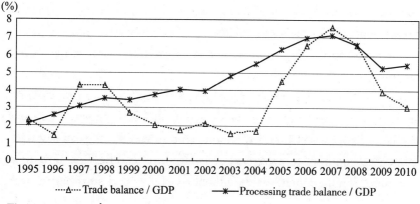

Figure 3. 1　China's trade balance takes over an increasing percentage of the GDP

The fact that the outward development mode has been challenged gradually became the supporting force for the adjustment to the industrial development mode. This, however, does not mean that China must abandon its external demand. The global economy of the future will definitely embrace both competition and cooperation. Global trade friction will become norm, and China must adapt to this situation.

The question of the "double deficit" in society and in the environment is also troubling China. Social deficit means that the fruit of global economic growth is enjoyed only by a small part of the population—that is, there is uneven distribution of wealth. The global reality is that while social welfare is generally on the rise, the income gap keeps widening. Hence a lot of people think that this kind of income distribution is unfair. And if we say that fairness means that people share the fruit of global economic development, then unfairness would mean that the laissez-faire mode of economic development is unsustainable. Therefore "sharing-type growth" is the realisation of the global sharing of the fruit of economic development.

Environmental deficits are also threatening the world of tomorrow. For instance, most of the surface water in China (with the exception of the water in the Qinghai-Tibet Plateau) cannot be directly used for drinking, and the areas threatened by acid rain are expanding. In short, China is under great pressure on the environmental front.

The repayment for the social and environmental deficits in effect is the increase in the cost of living and the cost of production. This means that we need to change the model and structure of economic growth, and also change people's way of living. The global economy of the future requires optimizing resources, sharing welfare, and achieving sustainable growth.

The social and environmental "double deficit" is an unavoidable hidden reef on the sea route of China's economic development. A careless mistake would cause China's economic ship to wreck. We can say that if China is to continue to progress, it must start to reflect on how to reduce this "double deficit" of the global economy, and start caring about the ecology and the environment, and also about narrowing the gap between the rich and the poor. In this regard, the "sharing-type economic growth" model may be the best solution. Economic policies can boost social productivity—that is, on the basis of upgrading the mode of economic development and achieving transition, build a mechanism for the sharing of social wealth, thereby enhance people's standard of living.

"Sustainability" by nature not only means the horizontal compatibility of people of the same period and region, but also the historic vertical compatibility of the present generation and the future generations in sharing resources. "Sustainable development" refers not only to the mode of production, but also the mode of living, working and behaviour. Human beings, especially the rich, must change their way of living in order to curb the deterioration of the ecology and the environment. Then we can achieve harmony between human beings and nature, between human beings and human beings, and between different generations.

Is "Selling Resources" Not as Good as "Selling Physical Labour"?

From the global perspective, some countries develop by "selling things" —for instance, Australia sells iron ore, while Saudi Arabia and Kuwait sell petroleum. Other countries develop by "selling physical labour" —for instance, China. 50% of China's foreign trade is processing trade, or in effect "selling physical labour" (See Figure 3.2).

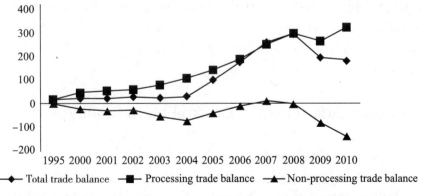

Figure 3. 2 **China's trade surplus mainly comes from processing trade** (US$ billion)

China's quality and cheap labour is an important foundation for the country's economic development. In other words, "selling physical la-

bour" is China's competitive advantage.

The difference between selling resource-intensive products and selling labour-intensive products is that a lot of resources will become less and less on consumption, and will one day be depleted. Natural resources like petroleum, trees and minerals belong to this category. Even money can flow into other people's purse through financial channels. Hence selling resources is non-renewable and unsustainable.

On the other hand, China's competitive economic factor—labour— is renewable and sustainable. Labour is not reduced on consumption, but rather the more the worker works, the more skillful he becomes— unskilled labour will become skilled labour. In other words, we can add value to human resources. Meanwhile, by virtue of reproduction, labour is sustainable.

In the process of "learning by doing", Chinese people add elements of wisdom into their work. At the same time, they add green economy, cyclic economy and low-carbon economy into their traditional mode of work, making the Chinese economic development model a sustainable model. The reason why China has exhibited huge power in the three decades of reform and opening-up is that China has chosen the correct competitive advantage, and coupled it with the right methods.

The history of China's industries proves that "selling physical labour" is China's most important competitive advantage. It is also the foundation of reform, an important channel for the Chinese economy to reap greater profit, and also the key to China's distinguished position in the world.

Structural Adjustment: "Dream Enters Reality"

"Goal" vs "Conditions"

China's success can be attributed to the move of the labour force from the traditional department to a modern department, to the constant deepening of the opening-up policy, and to the dynamic introduction of advanced productivity from the world.

The Yangtze River Delta and the Pearl River Delta—relatively af-

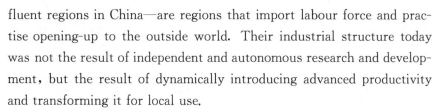

fluent regions in China—are regions that import labour force and prac-
tise opening-up to the outside world. Their industrial structure today
was not the result of independent and autonomous research and development, but the result of dynamically introducing advanced productivity
and transforming it for local use.

While China's growth pattern is not blessed with the foundation of
high technology, yet it was hugely successful! China's high productivity
has stunned the world!

China has inherited the transfer from the world industry and innovated this inheritance. Riding on economic globalisation, and spiced up
with Chinese wisdom, China has developed its own special industrial
system, and deepened the reform to ensure the smooth transference of
the labour force and the sustainability of the opening-up policy. Under
these conditions, and having gone through the reforms in the mode of e-
conomic growth, China will one day advance shoulder to shoulder with
developed industrial nations.

In order to reach its market-oriented economic development goals,
China must solve three problems. First, optimal allocation of resources
(harmony between human beings and nature). Second, a general rise in
welfare level (harmony among human beings). Third, the sustainability
of economic and social development (harmony between generations).
These are the basic principles that guide China's economic development.

In summing up the pattern of China's economic development, we
can group it into four major factors. First, the essential conditions for
China's economic development: the labour force is transferred from the
traditional department to the modernised department. Second, the ade-
quate conditions for China's economic development: constantly deepened
opening-up. Third, industry conditions for China's economic development: constantly ready to receive the transference of global industries to
enter into the industry from the high end. Fourth, the systemic conditions for China's economic development: system innovation provides as-
surance for the three processes mentioned above.

Economic globalisation, structural adjustments to global industries
under the conditions of the aggressive development of high technology

and financial development, active developments of multinational corporations, and the impact of the shortage of world resources—they all bring opportunities and challenges to China.

The focus of adjustments in China's economic growth model and structural reforms is to position China in the global economy—from a major economic country to an economic power. For this purpose, China adjusts its mode of economic growth and structural reform, and in the process continues to enhance the depth of reform and opening up, to balance external trade, to grasp the direction of reform in the financial industry and investment system, and to carry out the choice of development model, and the adjustment of trade.

At present, the development trend of China's reform and opening-up is in line with China's search for more effective allocation of resources, enhancement of welfare, and the sustainability of development—against the background of global economic imbalance.

China stands against the background of changing demands inside and outside the country. In the post-crisis age, China's industry development model and the adjustment of economic structure are based on the longing for survival, and then starting to make adjustments. China will constantly receive the transfer of global assets to carry out entry into high technology and local innovation. This will avoid blindly following the crowd on the path of development on the road to China's economic development.

China is busy adapting to the external environment. It will actively abide by the international rules in a bid to occupying an advantageous position in the trading system. On the basis of a full understanding or its industrial flexibility, strengths and weaknesses, China can create a high-end platform for the adjustments to the industrial structure.

Meanwhile, the adjustments to China's economic development model are dynamic, and a perpetual process. It is a means to achieve a production goal, rather than a long-term goal. There is no end to the adjustment to the economic development model. There was no ending in the past, and this kind of ending does not exist today or tomorrow. We should look at it as a dynamic process and give it permanence.

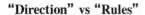

"Direction" vs "Rules"

China's economic structure adjustments have their footing on grasping the changes and trends in economic demands. This can be said to be the basic conditions for reforming China's economic models.

Hence in the face of adjustments to the reform on China's economic structure, we can borrow a common saying about traffic rules: "First, stop; second, look; third, pass. " In other words, first we ensure our survival. Then we stand securely. Finally we take a good look and implement adjustment. That is, we should not blindly adjust our economic and production structure without first taking a good look at the direction of change in terms of future demand.

In the last decade of the 20th century, a so-called "New Economy" appeared in the US. Basically this is a revolution in information technology against the background of economic globalisation, and an economy led by the high-tech industry and driven by the information technology revolution. This is mainly manifested in the development of the IT industry and network economy with information engineering technology at the core. According to statistics released in 2,000 by the US Ministry of Commerce's "Digital Economy Report 2000", 30% of the GDP in the US from 1995 to 1999 came from the IT industry.

When the "New Economy" appears, people cast their sight on IT and network with engineering technology at the core. But they have neglected one issue—another great US invention—financial derivatives. Up to 2005, the financial services industry already accounted for 20.4% of the GDP in the US. Indeed, technology engineering and financial engineering had become the parallel drivers in the US economy.

Through globalisation, these two projects spread to other parts of the world on a large scale. Globalisation is actually the unification of the markets and the unification of market game rules. These two unifications, from the technical point of view, helped the IT industry to go out to the world. From the financial point of view, they helped to promote financial derivatives worldwide, securitising everything.

It was precisely the latter that got into trouble, throwing the global economy off balance. The production of wealth and the allocation of wealth were distorted, resulting in wealth vaporisation. The question is: the risks in a virtual economy cannot be eliminated—they can only be transferred. The various risks generated by the US virtual economy were quickly transferred to the whole world through this big ship of globalisation.

Now, the US economic crisis is gradually dissipating after the "double dip", but is the lifestyle of over-spending still lingering in the new generation of Americans? If the answer is yes, then China's industrial structure can remain what it is. But if there is a fundamental shift in the US mode of spending, then the situation will be completely different—China's economic structure will definitely be adjusted.

"Opponent" vs "Strategy"

Since the advent of the new century, as international division of labour changed from industry to intra-industry division of labour, and then to division of labour within a product, there appeared in Asia vertical and horizontal systems of division of labour and a regional production and supply network. This is gradually taking shape.

After 2001, with the bursting of the US IT industry bubble as an important turning point, the international industry transfer process underwent new changes. After the 1980s, developed countries like the US saw their fast developing high-end manufacturing starting to expedite their outgoing transfer and investment.

At this stage, we see the further deepening and diminishing of the adjustment to the international division of labour mechanism. Wintelism rapidly spread to the whole world, and the adjustment to the division of labour in the manufacturing industry and the industrial transfer process have deepened to within the industry or within the product. Based on the different production tasks and procedures within the same product, demands are injected, and different production tasks and procedures are allocated to different countries or territories with different competitive advantages.

The basis of international division of labour is a shift from considering a country's competitive advantage in one final product, to the competitive advantage of one product in a specific task within the production value chain. From this, the concepts of "Made in the World" and "Global Value Chain" arose.

The diminishing of international division of labour means that more industries or production tasks are now in the process of international industrial transfer. Economies such as Europe, US, Japan, Hong Kong of China, Singapore, Korea and Taiwan of China are increasingly turning to high value-added capital-intensive or technology-intensive production or processing. On the other hand, they are transferring low value-added labour-intensive production and processing tasks to other countries on a large scale.

China's competitive advantage in labour costs and economic scale, as well as the system and policy advantages formed during the reform and opening-up period in the 1990s, coupled with the holistic impact of China's entry into WTO in 2001, made China the world's largest recipient of the new round of international industrial transfer.

China's rapid growth in the first decade of this century could be mainly attributed to the vertical division of labour system in Asia, and the regional trade relationships that serve this system. This is also attributable to the East Asia – China – Europe/US "tripartite trading model". In the new round of adjustment process in this international division of labour system, the Asian region has gradually become a unified supply chain network in the global economy. In this network, China is the final processing and packaging centre, whereas Japan, the Newly-industrialised Asian Economies and other ASEAN countries are the suppliers for capital products and middle products (See Figure 3. 3).

In the face of the post-crisis era and the adjustment and upgrading of China's industrial structure, if we take the labour-intensive type as the starting point and the low-end industrial chain entry as the basis, then China's competitive opponent is the new type of industrialised economies, such as Indonesia, Thailand, Malaysia and other Southeast Asian countries, or countries in Latin America and North Africa. When the industrial structure is truly adjusted to having the production of top-end products as the core, and with high-end technology forming an industrial cluster, then what China needs to really take note of is that its

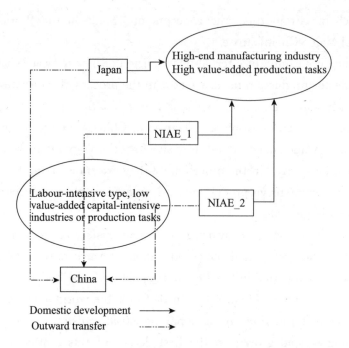

Figure 3. 3　International transfer of labour-intensive production tasks since the turn of the century

competitors are no longer the developing countries, but the developed e-conomies.

Among the emerging economies under the low labour cost model, China knows both itself and others. China knows how to tackle competition with low cost expansion and economies of scale. But in the face of competition from developed countries like the US in high-end industries, China will face certain difficulties, because it may not be able to discern the opponents' tricks and competitive paths. When developed countries use product standards, technical hurdles and green hurdles to wage a trade war, China will not be able to use low cost expansion to counter these. This is because when the competition is on high-end products, the price factor is only of secondary importance.

Therefore, given China's reform in its economic model and adjustment in industrial structure, when faced with competition from developed countries, China will have to find its own way. When China was faced with the escalating anti-dumping, anti-subsidy and protective

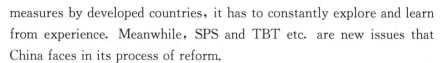

measures by developed countries, it has to constantly explore and learn from experience. Meanwhile, SPS and TBT etc. are new issues that China faces in its process of reform.

The change of opponents and competitive model is both the driving force for China's reform, and also a challenge. The higher the industrial structure and the level of competition are, the stronger the opponents are.

On the cost of labour, China in the past could compete with countries like Vietnam and the Philippines. But when the industrial structure is raised to competing with economies like the US and Germany, then the competitive platform and competitive environment will be fundamentally changed. We can say that China's direction in adjusting its industrial structure is correct, but the future road of competition will be arduous.

"Flexibility" vs "Choice"

Economic theories have it that any industry or product has two kinds of elasticities: price elasticity and income elasticity. Price elasticity shows the relationship between price changes and sales volume. A little change in price will result in a big change in sales. This means that there is a large price elasticity, otherwise it is small. On the other hand, income elasticity shows the relationship between income changes and sales volume. Similarly, a little change in income will result in a big change in sales. This again shows that there is a large income elasticity, otherwise it is small.

Some products have high price elasticity while others have low price elasticity. There are products called "Giffen Products" such as rice. If a bowl of rice costs $1, people eat one bowl. When the price drops to $0.5, people still eat one bowl. When it rises to $1.5, people still eat one bowl. Hence this kind of product does not have much elasticity. On the other hand, the more sophisticated the product is, the larger the elasticity is, and the larger the price elasticity is, the larger the income elasticity is.

China's trade surplus mainly arose from the trade in final processing of consumer products. High-tech products with large product flexibility account for only a minor percentage. According to one research report, after China's entry into WTO, the domestic content of export commodities was 50%, while the domestic content of high-tech products was only 30%.

One scholar found that processing trade and foreign investment enterprises were not the main motivating factor for the growing complexity of China's export commodities. Rather, the main reason for the upgrade of the export structure is the accumulation of labour capital as well as the tax concessions granted by the Government to the high-tech zones.

Let us categorise all products by their degree of technology intensity into four types labour and resource intensive products, and low-, medium-and high-technology-intensive products. Table 3.1 shows China's trade surplus during the decade from 2000 to 2010, and we can see that there has always been a surplus for labour-and-resource-intensive products, as well as low-technology-intensive products. This surplus is actually growing fast. In 2010, the trade surplus for labour-and-resource-intensive products amounted to US $ 336.2 billion, while the surplus for low-technology-intensive products reached US $ 124 billion.

Table 3.1　　**Trade Balance Structure for Chinese Products** (US $ billion)

	2000	2005	2006	2007	2008	2009	2010
Labour-and-resource-intensive type	64.9	171.9	217.8	264.3	299.7	269.5	336.2
Low-technology-intensive type	9.4	36.3	66.7	101.6	136.9	74.5	124.0
Medium-technology-intensive type	−8.3	−2.6	13.1	42.2	71.6	41.3	35.7
High-technology-intensive type	−20.8	−7.4	7.7	34.5	69.6	46.6	62.8

Source: Computed on the basis of data from the Unctad trade database.

We can see from Table 3.1 that the labour-and-resource-intensive products and low-technology-intensive products are the main source of China's trade surplus. The production of these products depends on the domestic labour force and raw materials, and most of these products have low elasticity. Meanwhile, medium-and-high-technology products

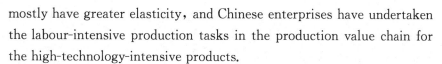

mostly have greater elasticity, and Chinese enterprises have undertaken the labour-intensive production tasks in the production value chain for the high-technology-intensive products.

From the technical composition of Chinese export commodities, we can draw a conclusion that when the income of European countries and the US is affected, what people give up first is definitely not the low elasticity daily necessities such as rice, but the high elasticity or so-called high-end products.

For instance, people need to wear shoes. When they have lots of money, they can wear prestigious Italian shoes. When they don't have much money, they will shift to quality and cheap shoes made in China.

Under these circumstances, the more sophisticated the product is, the larger the elasticity is, and the greater the impact is. Following the financial crisis, many toy factories in Guangdong closed down. Research data show that the factories that closed down first were those making high-technology toys. On the other hand, factories producing plastic and woolly toys survived the impact. Why? This is because kids need toys, and there is no elasticity in this. But whether they play with high-technology toys or low end woolly toys depends on the income level of the parents.

So we should never neglect the elasticity of products, especially in the context of the Chinese economy under reform. We can say that China's past success can be attributed to its deep understanding of the industries and the elasticity of its products. Hence a clear awareness of the reform in economic model, and the importance of industrial flexibility in the adjustment of industrial structure, is a must.

"Disadvantage" vs "Advantage"

In economics, the Cannikin Law states that the amount of water that a wooden bucket can hold is determined not by the long planks but the short planks. Hence we are not comparing competitive advantages of how far we can pull the industry, but comparative disadvantages that restrain the industry's development. Sometimes "comparative disadvantage" is all that matters. So it is important that we strengthen our disadvantages.

For a long time, the aggregated export growth of the Asian supply chain network (represented by China) has been in direct proportion to the growth in demand by the US and European markets. In the new century, there has been a significant growth in demand for external goods. From 2000 to 2008, the US's import demands accounted for 15.4% of the GDP, far higher than the 11.9% in the 1990s. The increased demand by the US and European markets created larger space for export growth among the Asian supply chain network.

As China is gradually becoming the processing and packaging centre for final products among the Asian supply chain network, the country has become an important platform for the final products that Asia exports to the US and European markets. As a result, China is gradually replacing other Asian economies as the main supplier of final products for the US and European markets, including the supply of final consumer products and investment products.

Take the US market as an example. Among the consumer products imported into the US since 1991, Asia accounts for about 40% all along. Of this 40%, China's contribution increased from 8.2% in 1991 to 27.1% in 2009 (See Figure 3.4 and Figure 3.5). Meanwhile, the percentage of consumer products exported by other Asian economies to the US has been steadily dropping (See Figure 3.6). The rising demand by the US and European markets, together with China replacing other Asian economies in the US and European markets, has driven the dramatic growth in Chinese exports since 2000.

China differs from the rest of the world in its business model: the Western world pursues the maximisation of profit, but China pursues the maximisation of its global market share, using low profit as a means and even at the expense of zero profit. This is China's greatest characteristic. Although this path is unsustainable, yet it will eventually transform China's mode of production.

The high-tech realm may be the short plank in the bucket for China. Yet in the product life cycle, high tech nology may not be the means to raise prices. Sometimes high technology can contribute to China's other competitive weapon—low costs.

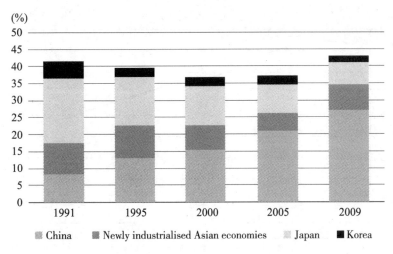

Figure 3. 4   China accounts for a growing percentage in the export of consumer products to the US

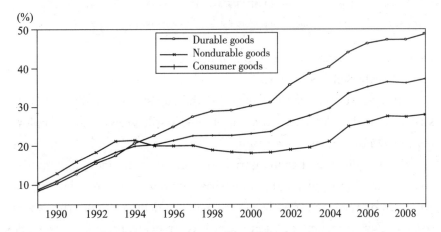

Figure 3. 5   US imports a constantly growing amount of consumer products from China

China's economic model reform and industrial structure adjustment have given more concern to the high-tech realm. This will enable China to take greater advantage of advanced technology, which has been a "relative disadvantage" for China. Low costs plus advanced technology will become China's killer weapon after its industrial upgrade. Different from other countries, China is able to develop both upstream and downstream simultaneously in the value chain. China can even uplift the va-

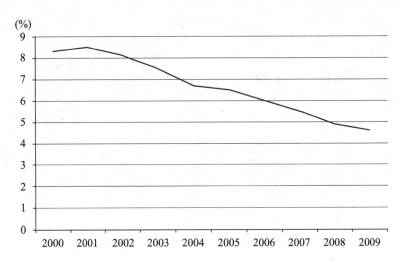

Figure 3. 6　Export of consumer products by Asian economies outside China is steadily decreasing

Source: Based on statistics from IMF "Regional Economic Outlook" (Asia and Pacific) and "Chinese Macro Economic Analysis and Forecast Report (First Quarter, 2012)".

lue chain to command a wider global market.

"Distribution" vs "Growth"

At present, one of the trends for the adjustment to the industrial structure in the global economy is: there is still growth, but employment may not increase as a result.

As the adjustment to industrial structure becomes more high grade, and as the degree of capital intensity continues to rise, the organic structure of the industries becomes higher and higher, but the labour content that each unit of capital can accommodate becomes lower and lower. Since the 1990s, growth in employment in China has far lagged behind the expansion of the total size of the economy. This means that the employment-generation potential of the expansion of the total economy is on the decline (See Figure 3. 7).

With the perfection of China's labour market and the rise in the negotiation power of the workforce, real wages are constantly on the rise, and its gap with the labour productivity rate becomes narrower and narrower. This has resulted in "skilled workers" replacing the low-end workforce. From the perspective of different industries, the employ-

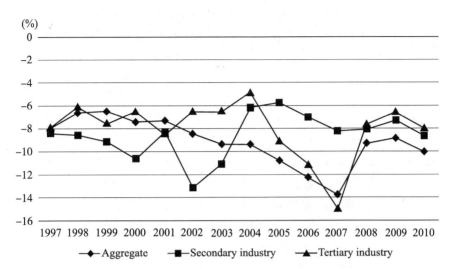

Figure 3. 7 Difference between Employment Growth Rate and GDP Growth Rate

Source: "Chinese Macro Economic Analysis and Forecast Report (First Quarter, 2012)".

ment-creation effect from the aggregate growth of China's secondary industry is lower than that from the tertiary industry.

How many people among the total workforce of an economy can actually adapt to high-tech industries? If only a relatively small percentage of the workforce can adapt to high-tech industries, then this will happen: while there is no significant increase in employment, there may be growth in the total income of the workforce. Correspondingly, the not-too-many workers who can adapt to the structural adjustment of the industry will enjoy a significantly higher income. Meanwhile, the majority of the workers who cannot adapt to the changes will also enjoy an elevated income.

In an imperfect labour market, the lack of employment opportunities makes it difficult for workers to have a higher negotiating power. The market is highly motivated to adjust the industrial structure, but this kind of adjustment through the market cannot result in the even distribution of income—rather, it will only widen the gaps in income distribution, resulting in the aggravation of the problem of employment income and family income. This in turn will create serious social problems. This is the social cost of structural adjustment. Some people call it "the ceiling of the social cost of structural adjustment".

This is the reality faced by China's reform process. While there is economic growth, there is no employment growth. And this is accompanied by social problems created by serious unevenness in income distribution. This is an inevitable problem inherent in the reform of China's economic model and the adjustment of industrial structure.

How to resettle the majority of the workers who cannot adapt to the industrial structure adjustment process? The Chinese Government is very concerned about this issue. In fact, the Chinese Government needs to map out strategies to deal with the social costs of reform. Otherwise this will become "the sword of Damocles" to the Chinese economy that is charging ahead in full steam.

"Flow" vs "Ending"

In the age of economic globalisation, if one country can really control the flow of global resources and the flow of global economic output, then this country will have a bigger say in setting the game rules of the global economy based on its control over the double flow of resources and production output. Its interests will then enjoy more fundamental protection.

The decisive resource in the 21st century is the direction of flow of human resources and financial resources—on which the trend of future productivity depends. And the global economic output is hinged on the basic products needed for people's livelihood, and the high-tech products that will drive people's future.

During 1997 and 1998, the Asian financial crisis created chaos in the outskirts of global finance. However, the global financial centres, such as Wall Street and London, emerged unharmed by the allocation of global resources. Their demands are still growing. Amidst the chaos of the entire Southeast Asian production system, its demands can only be satisfied by China. As China enjoyed political and economic stability at that time, the demands of the world and large amounts of direct investments came to China. Thus China became the factory of the world—this is actually the result of Wall Street allocating resources. To put simply, though the demand is from the US and Europe, the FDI is the world's. When the two merge in

Wall Street, China became the "world factory".

The subprime crisis of the US in 2008 sent the world's financial centres into chaos. Its function in allocating global resources was damaged to some extent. This gave China the opportunity to allocate global resources from the perspective of China's interests, which builds a high-end platform for the adjustment of industrial structure.

If what "goes out" is commodities, the country can only call itself a big country. It is only when capital really "goes out" that the country can call itself a power.

In terms of "capital going out", China has just made its first step. In recent years, China has been actively cooperating with African and South American countries, to carry out the process of autonomously allocating resources in the Chinese style and with Chinese characteristics. This will provide sustained protection for the strong growth of China's domestic economy.

In recent years, China's direct external investments have been growing rapidly (See Table 3. 2). In 2010, the amount of direct investments accounted for 5. 1% of the global amount, occupying the 5th place in the world, and overtaking Japan and UK, gaining top place among the developing countries. As a result, China became a country that has over US $ 50 billion in direct investments when it is still at "middle income level".

Table 3. 2 Outflow of Foreign Direct Investment for Developing Economies from 2000 to 2008 (US$ billion, %)

Region/country	2000	2001	2002	2003	2004	2005	2006	2007	2008
Africa	1.5	−2.7	0.3	1.2	1.9	1.1	7.1	10.6	9.3
Latin America and the Caribbeans	60.0	32.2	14.7	15.4	27.5	32.8	63,6	51.7	63.2
Asia	82.2	47.1	34.7	19.0	83.4	83.6	144.4	223.1	220.1
West Asia	1.5	−1.2	0.9	−2.2	7.4	15.9	23.9	48.3	33.7
East Asia	72.0	26.1	27.6	14.4	59.2	54.2	82.3	111.2	136.1
China	0.9	6.9	2.5	−0.2	1.8	11.3	21.2	22.5	52.2

Cont.

Region/country	2000	2001	2002	2003	2004	2005	2006	2007	2008
South Asia	0.5	1.4	1.7	1.4	2.1	1.5	14.9	17.8	18.2
Southeast Asia	8.2	20.8	4.6	5.4	14.7	12.0	23.3	45.8	32.1
Developing economies	143.8	76.7	49.7	35.6	112.8	117.5	215.3	285.5	292.7
World	1,244.5	764.2	539.5	561.1	813.1	778.7	1,396.9	2,146.5	1,857.7
Percentage of developing economies	11.6	10.0	9.2	6.3	13.9	15.1	15.4	13.3	15.7

Source: UN Trade Development Conference, "2006 World Investment Report" and "2009 World Investment Report".

The rapid growth of China's foreign direct investments is actually caused by the internal vitality of China's economic development. According to the "Two-gap Model" propounded by the economic advisor of the World Bank, Prof. Hollis B. Chenery of Harvard University, China at the start of the reform and opening-up policy faced the shortage of savings and the shortage of foreign exchange. In the face of this "two-gap" problem, the control of foreign investments can effectively prevent the enlargement of these gaps. With the development of the Chinese economy and the increase in foreign exchange reserve, there are an excess of domestic savings and an excess of foreign exchange reserve—the so-called "double excess" pattern. This calls for the Government to carry out necessary adjustments to the economic policy, and progressively relax its control over foreign direct investments.

In today's global economic situation, if we can control the flow of resources, we will be able to set the game rules for global business. Whoever sets the standards for the products will be powerful. China's continued deepening of the reform and opening-up policy builds the foundation for China to set the game rules for the global economy. China is abiding by and executing the game rules of the global economy. And riding on the rights bestowed by various international economic organisations, China will protect its rights given to it in the process of economic globalisation. Of course, it is important to adapt to the global "game" rules, but if we can participate in setting the rules and using the rules, and can realise the interests of China in the global economy in the context of the rules, it will be an even better scenario. This is because rules determine how the game is played. So whoever sets the rules will have the last word.

In the process of reform in the economic model, China will progressively care about, and take part in, the setting of the game rules of global economy. In the setting of the rules, China will have a say about its interests, and will have a stronger voice. China will join hands with other countries to overcome the negative impact of economic imbalance, and to further enjoy the benefits of economic globalisation.

Part 4

Imbalance and Balance

"To the same question, 100 economists will give 101 answers." This merely shows that economists have very diverse views on various issues. However, to the statement "the global economy today is out of balance", all economists will unprecedentedly and unanimously agree.

"The global economy is out of balance", and "the global economy needs to resume its balance" —these statements seem to be the consensus of economists. However, they will have different views regarding "who to take responsibility to restore the balance" and "how the global economy should restore its balance".

We can say that to the world today, restoring the balance of the global economy is not just the realm of analysis of economists, as it has well gone beyond pure economic analysis. The issue is interspersed with interest scrambling, political pressure, and social reform. This is perhaps the largest and most complicated, but also the most important and most imperative, issue in global economy today.

The stage for the re-balancing of the global economy is ready, and the curtain for the balancing act is up. Who will be the protagonist in this show? What role will China play? Re-balancing is a process of adjustment, and a process of reform. Adjustment incurs costs, and reform incurs loss. The road to re-balancing the global economy will be long and difficult, and never plain-sailing.

Global Economy: "Imbalance" and "Re-balance"

For many years, people have in general recognised that the global economy is out of balance. They also recognise that this "imbalance" was formed in the process of economic globalisation. Hence, there is the consensus that "after losing balance, the economy needs to re-balance". However, in the past three decades, the content of "imbalance" and "balance" has gone through significant changes.

"This imbalance" is not "that imbalance"?

With the latest developments in economic globalisation, the concept of imbalance of the global economy has in the global context acquired a brand new understanding and interpretation. In other words, the word "imbalance" no longer means what it used to mean. This has had enormous impact on China, with negative effects on the country's development.

The term "imbalance of the global economy" is not a new concept. It has been widely discussed in the last century. People have even stated that it is necessary to re-balance the global economy before the global e-conomy can achieve sustainability.

At that time, when people mentioned the imbalance of the global e-conomy, what they referred to was that there are rich countries and poor countries—that is about the relationship between the north and the south. "Imbalance" meant that there is imbalance between the rich and the poor in the north-south economic relationship, and there is poverty inside affluence. And "balance" meant that developed countries had the responsibility to render assistance to the developing countries. In other words, the question is how developing countries should develop. It is only when developing countries have developed themselves that the entire global village and the entire global economy can enjoy comprehensive development. Hence in the 1990s there was the implementation of a millennium anti-poverty plan.

Under these conditions, things should be very favourable to China.

115

This is because China is the world's largest developing country, and has probably the largest number of poverty-stricken communities. We can actually say that the poverty-stricken communities in China and India add up to more than half of the poverty-stricken communities in the world. If the problem of poverty in these two countries is solved, then half the poverty-related problems in the world will be solved.

China's reform and opening-up has gained the approval and support of the entire world—from the standpoint of alleviating poverty. Hence when China started its reform and opening-up plan, the entire world applauded and rendered strong support. When you need capital, capital will come. When you need markets, markets will become available. When you need technology, the necessary technology transfer will take place. All of these have one single purpose—to fight poverty on earth, and to achieve balance and sustainability. All the countries have recognised China as having the obligation to free other developing countries from poverty. Hence China at that time was in a very favourable position.

Into the 21st century, the global economy is still out of balance, but people mean something else when they talk about the global economy losing balance. In fact the term they use has changed too—not to balance the out-of-balance global economy, but to re-balance the out-of-balance global economy.

This imbalance refers to the imbalance of the recurrent international income and expenditure between developed countries and emerging market economy countries. This recurrent imbalance in the accounts has resulted in the unsustainability of the global economy. "Re-balance" means balancing the imbalance of the international balance of payment— that is, emerging market economies need to eradicate the huge trade surpluses. Apparently, China today is one of the countries with the biggest trade surplus, the biggest exports, and the largest foreign reserve. The most prominent trade surplus and trade deficit in the world are in China and the US.

Under these circumstances, the developed countries are demanding that China reduce its trade surplus, in order to contribute to the re-balance of the world. This is relatively unfavourable to the overall development of China. What this concept tells you is that the issue of "balance" between the rich and the poor has become secondary in terms of priority, and now the task at hand is to "re-balance" the recurrent account of the world. People think that the emerging market economies, especially China, should drastically reduce their trade surpluses in order to help the developed countries, especially the US, to overcome their trade deficits.

We can say that re-balancing the global economy to achieve benefit sharing and sustainable growth is the theme of the global economy, and the issue of balancing between the rich and the poor is no longer the key issue on the agenda of the current international economic management and cooperation. The development issue that we can still mention is no longer balancing the development of the global economy, but green development. Under these circumstances, the conflicts and contradictions in the global economy will become prevalent.

"Phenomenon" ≠ "Nature"?

The imbalance of the global economy is the imbalance of the allocation of global resources and the allocation of income. We have pointed out earlier that the imbalance of the global economy is manifested in the imbalance of the recurrent international income and expenditure between developed countries and emerging market economy countries. Here the focus of global attention is the trade surplus and trade deficit between China and the US.

However, from the standpoint of reality, this is also the imbalance of domestic economic structure of developed countries and emerging market economy countries, as well as the imbalance between the real economy development and virtual economic development. And finally, this is the imbalance in the development of global finance.

Although some Western scholars are of the view that the international economic crisis in 2008 was caused by the abovementioned "global economic imbalance", yet fundamentally the international financial crisis in 2008 was caused by the US over-developing its financial system and virtual economy, resulting in a serious imbalance between the real economy and virtual economy.

The direct cause of the serious imbalance in the current accounts of China and the US is actually the US economic model that encourages over-spending. The global economy is demand-driven. The excessive demand of the US for global commodities resulted in East Asian countries, mainly China, over-producing and over-supplying. What I must point out is that the pre-condition for this imbalance is that the US took the initiative to upgrade its industrial structure to one that has real estate and finance as the main economic pillar. The US also drove its economic growth by encouraging its people to excessively spend on credit. The result was that the virtual domestic economy over-expanded to such an extent that it de-coupled from the country's real economy and operated on its own, thus eventually causing the crisis.

So the basic reason for the imbalance of the global economy is related to the structural issues within different countries, and the systemic root was the international currency system driven by the US dollar. The result was that the total demand in the global economy was unable to digest the total supply, and this was manifested in the global economic imbalance.

The Patient Has Flu, But Asks Others to Take Medicine

At present, making adjustments to the global economic imbalance has become the core issue in the post-crisis global economy. However, long-term problems are not just caused by short-term reasons. In the rebalancing process of the global economy, any structural adjustments will have a profound impact on parties with vested interest, and also on the distribution of interests within the country. As a result, the parties with vested interest in the country will tend to adopt a boycott attitude, asserting great pressure on the relevant governments.

The biggest imbalance in the global economy is the imbalance between China and the US. Unfortunately, the US, to protect its own interests, is shirking its responsibility in re-balancing the global economy, putting the responsibility to balance the China-US trade on China, and even blaming the global economy imbalance on China.

As reported in the website of *The Daily Telegraph* in UK, US

Federal Reserve Chairman Prof. Ben Bernanke blamed China for risking "slowing down the growth rate of all the countries". Bernanke insisted that "Letting currencies similar to the RMB appreciate will pay the deposit for balancing the recurrent account of the global economy, and is the desired result for the long-term stability of the economic and financial system. "

This comment is actually the excuse of the US to put the responsibility of re-balancing the global economy on China. Indeed, this is like saying "I have flu, but you should take the medicine" — and will not do any good.

Excuse 1: China-US Trade Is Seriously out of Balance

The US has exaggerated the seriousness of the China-US trade imbalance.

First, the US exaggerated the actual difference in the current accounts between China and the US.

When using the traditional method to compute import and export trade, the current account merely reflects a country's import-export trade and investment income and expenditure. It does not take any consideration of the trade activities of multinational corporations. However, 60% of China's exports are completed by foreign companies.

It is well-known that in reality the trading between China and the US is that the US enterprises gradually retreat from their country's manufacturing industry, and move their production and processing units to China. Then they sell these commodities to China, US and the world. So large amounts of US assets are operating in China, and to a large extent this replaces the need to export to China. Here, multinational corporations play an important role. Hence, when calculating the trade imbalance between China and the US, it will be inappropriate to neglect this export amount and the activities of multinational corporations between China and the US. However, in the US statistics on trading with China, there is no consideration of the trading activities of the multinational corporations. Hence the trade imbalance between China and the US is exaggerated.

Moreover, there are a lot of unreasonable issues related to the US trade statistics—in terms of standards, scope, place of origin, transshipment trade and method of appreciation. All of these exaggerate the difference between the China and US current accounts. In actual fact, the greatest discrepancies in the calculation of trade balance between China and the US originated in the transshipment trading that China and the US were conducting through certain economies.

Second, in the allocation of benefits in China-US trading activities, the US has enjoyed more benefits.

On the one hand, it must be made clear that the trading structure between China and the US is complementary. The trades are mutually beneficial. China is a developing country, and the level of economic development is lower. When exporting to the US, China mainly takes advantage of the lower costs, and the products are mainly labour-intensive products. On the other hand, the US as a super power, has absolute advantage in terms of capital, technology and brand. As a result, the US is at an advantage in the allocation of trading benefits, and actually gathers most of the trading benefits. So we can say that there is imbalance in the allocation of trading benefits between China and the US.

In the global industry chain, China's role is mainly processing and assembling. These are not related to high technology, and the trading benefits are low. On the other hand, the US controls product research and development, marketing and service delivery. So we can say that US capital has a firm grasp of the right of control and allocation in the global industry chain. In the allocation of trade benefits between China and the US, American capital enjoys a higher percentage, and Chinese capital has a lower bargaining power in the allocation of benefits, and therefore reaps a smaller quota.

Hence although the China-US trading relationship is mutually beneficial and a win-win situation, yet there is serious imbalance when it comes to benefits allocation. We can say that the US receives more benefits. However, the US still stresses that it is treated in an imbalanced way, exaggerating the seriousness of the imbalance.

Excuse 2: RMB Should Drastically Appreciate in Order to Re-balance

"RMB exchange rate is under-valued→Chinese export commodities are cheap→China's trade surplus against the US continues to widen→US industries decline→US unemployment remains high" —this logic is generally accepted by the US. This has become an excuse for forcing the RMB to appreciate, and even for using the RMB exchange rate as a political tool for the US.

However, the reality of China-US trade and the trade by other emerging economies, as well as the history of trading between Japan and the US and between Germany and the US—all show that adjusting the currency exchange rates is not the panacea for adjusting trade imbalances.

The enormous trade surplus between China and the US is mainly due to structural issues such as US over-spending and China over-producing. We can further assert that it is caused by the international currency system driven by the US Dollar, rather than by the RMB exchange rate. We can say that when the US Dollar is still the leading force in the international currency system, it will be impossible for the US to maintain long-term foreign trade balance.

The US's own industry structure has decided on this fact: a trade surplus may not necessarily increase the US's employment, and a trade deficit may not necessarily decrease its employment. The US's trade deficit will increase its employment in the research and development, marine transport, marketing and financial areas. Of course, China and US's consumption and corporate governance need to be adjusted, in order to change the fragile balance in the global economy caused by China's over-production and the US's over-spending.

In the re-balancing process of the global economy, we must clearly see that the exchange rate factor is only one of the factors affecting international trade, and not the only factor, and not even a basic factor. Division of labour, comparative cost, endowment of essential factors, product differentials and overlapping demand, market competitiveness, international shift of capital, technological innovation and product innovation, product supply-demand relationships between related countries and regions—these are all factors that impact on the trend of international trading. When we analyse the trade imbalance between China and the US, we must not completely ignore the other factors and regard the exchange issue as the one and only one major issue. If we do so, we will be putting the cart before the horse.

On the other hand, we have mentioned earlier that the trade imbalance between China and the US is due to global industrial transfer, the upgrading of the US industry structure—moving the middle-to-low level production lines and the processing and packaging of goods in the global industry chain to China. This international trade imbalance cannot be changed merely by approving the drastic appreciation of the RMB.

From China's standpoint, the imbalance of the global economy is a normal occurrence in the process of globalisation. The US is the main beneficiary. Re-balancing is a long-term task, and China should bear a part of the responsibilities—through adjusting China's economic structure and reforming the mode of economic growth and upgrading the industries. We have very good reasons to believe that China's trade surplus will gradually diminish, and China will work hard to re-balance the global economy.

However, it seems that this is not the outcome that the US needs. The US neglects the long-term effects; rather, they hope that in the short term, appreciating the RMB will re-balance the global economy. The truth is that in the face of the US's weak domestic economy and high unemployment rate and debts, the US politicians need a scapegoat to release them from the political pressure that they face.

The appreciation of the RMB is a double-edged sword to the US economy and even to the global economy. The US Government and the US politicians know better than anybody that what they are doing now is pretending to be stupid, and politicising the issue of RMB exchange rate, so as to confuse the public. We can say that if the RMB really appreciates significantly, this will cause the US's import costs to rise and China's exports to fall. And this will deal a heavy blow on the global economy that is already out of balance. Then what people will get will not be a re-balanced economy, but even more dismal ruins.

From historical data and the experience of Japan and Germany, we know that the appreciation or depreciation of a currency has limited effect on adjusting trade income and expenditure. In the 1970s and

1980s, the US also put pressure on Germany and Japan to appreciate their currencies. However, in 2008, the US still had a trade deficit against Germany to US $ 42. 9 billion, and against Japan to US $ 72. 6 billion. From 2005 to 2008, the RMB appreciated fast against the US Dollar, and during the same period the trade deficit of the US against China grew by 21. 6% —the fastest in history so far. In 2009, the RMB to US Dollar exchange rate remained relatively stable, and the US to China trade deficit dropped by 16. 1%. Hence we can see that the RMB exchange rate is not the main factor for the US-China trade deficit. The real root of the US's illness is the country's own imbalances.

The drastic and rapid appreciation of the RMB will have negative impact on China—affecting the country's domestic macro-economic operations and the upgrading of the industry structure. Please look at the figures: suppose US $ 1 million enters China today, and exchanges into RMB 6. 3 million. Then you spend RMB 1. 3 million to buy a house, and put RMB 5 million in the bank to gain interest, waiting for the RMB exchange rate to appreciate to US $ 1 to RMB 5. This RMB 5 million will be changed back to US dollars, and there will be US $ 1 million. The question is: where does the cash accumulated come from? On the question of RMB exchange rate, we must not simply succumb to the pressure from the US. Rather, the reform of the mechanism that determines the RMB exchange rate should be based on the real situation of the Chinese economy itself. We need to be proactive and progressive, and move forward under control. This will ensure that the reform on China's economic development and the mode of economic development are well served.

Excuse 3: China Should Increase its Import of US Products

To improve the imbalance of China-US trade, and then to rebalance the global economy, the US proposed that on top of the RMB significantly appreciating, China should increase its import and consumption of US products. But can this really change the current imbalance of the China-US current accounts? The answer is there are still uncertainties.

When analysing this problem, we must first consider the trading pattern between China and the US. China is a developing country and the domestic consumer market is already in a situation where the supply is greater than the demand. If it is to step up its import of US consumer products, then some of the less competitive enterprises will close down, causing employees to lose their jobs and the workers' income to drop. As the domestic market shrinks and the people's income drops, and so does their spending power. Then China will reduce its need for imported products from the US. On the other hand, competitive enterprises will export their surplus products, but this does not solve the problem of trade imbalance.

This is the conclusion drawn under the condition that the US consumer goods are competitive in terms of pricing and function. In reality, in the consumer goods market, the consumer goods made in China are more competitive than the US goods. And if China is to import more of the investment goods, then this will on the one hand exacerbate the excessive production of some goods in China, resulting corporations to close down, people to lose their jobs and the demand for imports to drop. On the other hand, these additional investment goods will create new production capacity and product export capacity, which will in turn increase the trade deficit for developed countries. Hence even if China is forced to increase imports from the US, the result may not be the balance of trading surplus and deficit.

One of the main reasons for the China-US trade balance is the export control policy imposed on the competitive high technologies and products in the US. On the other hand, the medium to low end products are those that China also produces, and are those that China have a clear competitive advantage over. The China domestic market is already saturated, and there is no demand to import from the US.

In fact, the US is enjoying tremendous benefits from the China-US trade imbalance. Through importing quality and cheap products from China, the US is able to curb inflation, and consumers enjoy real concessions and savings, and reduced labour costs. At the same time, China is using the US dollars gained from the trade surplus to purchase US treasuries, giving the US considerable financial benefits. On the other hand, what China gets is merely US treasuries with electronic bookings, and even has to bear the foreign currency losses brought about by the depreciation of the US Dollar. Under these circumstances the US does not suffer any real loss. In fact it should admit that it is the beneficiary in the global economic imbalance.

"Role" and "Show" on the Global Economic Stage

The global economic imbalance is in reality a structural and systemic issue, and we cannot expect any short-term adjustments in the global context. On the other hand, if we allow this to develop further and let the situation worsen, the inevitable result will be the exacerbated imbalance and instability of the global economy, which is recovering from crisis. Hence the various parties to the imbalance, whether it be the developed economies or the emerging market countries, are all protagonists in the re-balancing of the global economy—they all need to bear their own responsibilities in the adjustment process. If any country merely hopes that other countries will make adjustments and does not take any action itself, there will not be any win-win situation.

Who to Bear the Cost for Global Imbalance?

In the face of the crisis of global economic imbalance spreading throughout the world, developed countries are proposing an economic re-balancing strategy with an aim to quickly escape from the crisis and revive their national economy.

The economic re-balancing strategy of the Western countries is this—the re-balancing of the global economy requires adjustment costs, and developed economies have the capability to transfer the costs of re-balancing adjustments to the emerging market economies through various economic and trade policies. The developed economies hope that the emerging market economies will bear the main costs for re-balancing the global economy, so that the developed economies will reap the benefits of global economic re-balance without suffering the pain of adjustment and transition. As China is a huge economy fast developing its export economy, and as it differs from developed countries in its systems and values, China is considered to be the main responsible party in the global economic imbalance.

Real economic re-balance will not just care for the balance of the current account and putting the focus of re-balancing on the realm of trade. Rather, the various parties to the imbalance should stand firm on their own economic structure and carry out optimisation of their industry structures. Reforming the existing international currency system is the energy for recovery from low inflation in the global economy. This will narrow the gap between the rich and the poor in various countries and territories, thereby realising the sustainability of the global economy. From a long-term perspective, it is only when economic growth is based on internal balance and external balance that it can become sustainable. If we merely stress the demand of developed countries or the supply of emerging market economies as the driving force, we will not achieve any ideal outcome. The policy of "drinking poison to quench thirst" will only exacerbate the global economic imbalance, resulting in all the parties becoming losers in the game.

In conclusion, global economic re-balance should be the goal and direction of the concerted effort of all the countries. For instance, the US as a developed economy should change its own spending mode, reduce pre-spending, increase savings, and lower the fiscal deficit. Europe and Japan should reform their domestic economy and structures, increase domestic demand and economic growth rate, advocate technological reform, and improve the potentials for economic development. Meanwhile, emerging market countries such as China should change their mode of economic growth, upgrade their industry structure, and in the case of China, expedite the marketisation of the RMB exchange rate. The special positions of China and the US in the global economic imbalance require that both parties play a bigger role and take greater responsibilities in the process of adjustment in the global economic re-balancing.

To solve the problem of global economic imbalance requires all the countries and territories to cooperate and render mutual support, rather than putting the responsibility on others. Global economic re-balancing is the responsibility of all the countries in the world, and it must be achieved through the sustained and sincere international cooperation among the key imbalanced countries.

Part 5

China: A Role in Coordination and Governance

"Crime" and "Punishment" in Global Governance

People often say that the real world is colourful, busy and complex, but probably not as captivating as the utopia depicted in poetry. Yet being "real" has its own attractions, charm and unpredictable landscape. The world changes drastically, and after some vicissitude, maybe utopia is on the horizon.

In this real world driven by interests, there is cut throat competition among countries, there is constant allocation of interests, transfer of status, and adjustment of patterns... friends and foes are perhaps just a step apart. In various countries, these seemingly complex relationship changes are tied to one thread, and this is "national interest". As famous German Chancellor Otto Von Bismarck said in total frankness, "A country does not have permanent friends, only permanent interests. " This may seem too cold-hearted, but it is also very true. "Reality" looks to be chilly and lacks human warmth.

The subprime crisis originating from the US soon spread, and finally evolved to become the most serious global financial crisis after the War. Not only did it hit the economy of various countries, but it also impacted on the "one super power and many powers" global pattern that evolved from the former USSR. The US domestic economy was worrying, and its strong position was undermined to some extent. The European powers were also veiled by the shadow of crisis, and many countries in the Euro Zone found themselves in the quagmire of debt, unable to free themselves. In stark contrast to the above, the emerging market economies, represented by China, India and Brazil, gradually became the new "engine" of global economic recovery and development, by virtue of their steady economic growth rate and economic vibrancy.

In the global ranking of economies, Brazil was ranked 6th, with the scale of its economy overtaking UK for the first time. Similar to Brazil's economic development, the emerging market economies of China, India, Russia and South Africa were on the rise too. In 2009, Russia and South Africa displaced UK and Canada to gain a place among the world's top 10 economies. In 2012, India also became the world's 10th largest economy (See Table 5.1).

Table 5.1   2012 Rankings of Global Economic Strength

Ranking	1	2	3	4	5	6	7	8	9	10
Country	US	China	Japan	Germany	France	Brazil	UK	Italy	Russia	India

Source: Centre for Economic and Business Research.

Emerging market economies are playing a more and more prominent role on the global stage, by virtue of their growth in economic strength and rise in international status. After the crisis, in the foreseeable future, developed countries and developing countries (in particular the conflicts among the emerging market economies) will engage in power struggles, economic battles, and the disintegration and re-establishment of alliances. These incidents will be re-enacted in even wider stages. And the adjustments and changes in the management mechanism of the global economy will become the focus of gaming between the two parties.

Governance Mechanism: Can You "Change Faces"?

Without instruments, it is difficult to draw squares and circles. Without rules and regulations, the world will not be the Garden of Eden; it will just be the chaotic "medieval age". To ensure that the global economy operates steadily and healthily, various members of the international community has built up a comprehensive system of rules and codes of practice. This will make the macro economic policies of various countries better coordinated, so that these countries will be able to take joint precautionary measures and to jointly tackle the global economic issues. This system, complete with its rules and regulations, and codes of practice, has come to be known as "Global Economy Governance Mechanism".

The global economy governance mechanism after the Second World War was set up and driven by the Western developed countries, and naturally safeguards the interests of the leaders. This governance mechanism has all along been used up to now, and embraces the global trade management system represented by the World Trade Organisation (WTO), the global finance management system represented by the International Monetary Fund (IMF) and the World Bank (WB), as well as meeting mechanism for the heads of state of Western developed countries. The G7 Summit, a mechanism that gathers the leaders of the seven countries in the 1970s to solve crises and resurrect the Western economy, is a typical case. Under this global economy governance mechanism, a lot of developing countries can only work in accordance with the rules of the developed countries, that is, sacrifice their own selfish rules in favour of national interest.

Since the end of the Second World War, all the countries that have a command of the direction of flow of global resources and the direction of flow of global economic outputs actually possess the power to lead the global economy. Only these countries qualify as really powerful countries. For a rather long period after the Second World War, only Western countries like the US and European countries were on the list.

In the 1970s, the US controlled the flow of petroleum resource through pegging the US Dollar to petroleum. Western developed countries led by the US controlled (through the developed financial market) the market price and market flow of important basic products that impact on people's livelihood—these products include food and mining resources.

Regarding the pricing mechanism for petroleum, before the first oil crisis in the 1970s, oil prices were in the hands of the seven sisters in the Western world. Then the pricing authority for petroleum fell into the hands of OPEC.

Since the two futures markets of New York and London gradually became the authority that sets the international prices of petroleum, the pricing right was again transferred to Wall Street and financial city London.

After the Second World War, the US always regarded overseas students as a reserve pool of talent. They kept revising the immigration laws and attracted a large batch of overseas students. Moreover, the US also approved a proposal to provide scholarships for students and scholars to study there. The budget for general education for all increases each year by tens of billions of US dollars. World renowned universities like Harvard and Princeton attract overseas students to study there through generous grants, scholarships and concessionary loans, and the amount accounts for nearly one-third of foreign students globally. 25% of the overseas students settle in the US after graduation, and contribute to the national pool of talents. In the US National Academy of Sciences, foreign scholars account for 22% of the total. Among the US citizens who have won Nobel Prizes, 35% of them were born outside the US. In the 21st century, the US takes advantage of its robust national strength to direct the flow of talents and capital, and command the future development direction of the high-tech product market, thereby determining the development trend of future productivity. The US human resources policy has reaped abundant results. Up to 2009, there were 796 Nobel Prize winners, and among them 315 had US citizenship, or 39.57% of the total.

Through controlling the pricing of strategic commodities, talents and the flow of capital, developed countries tightly control the right to set the rules of the global economy, thereby commanding the "high grounds" of international economy competition, and the right of initiative in the volatile economy. The global economy governing mechanism set up after the Second World War is actually where the Western developed countries set the "game rules".

With the passage of time, the global pattern is constantly in a flux of change. The developing countries are growingly powerful. On the other hand, after the global financial crisis triggered by the US subprime crisis, the power of the Western developed countries was undermined, and the emerging market economies represented by the BRICS countries rose quickly to prominence and started to assume a position of balance against the developed countries, thereby setting the scene for developing countries to play a bigger role on the global stage.

While the gloomy shadow of the global financial crisis still lingers, the alarm for the developing countries to change the unreasonable international economic order is ringing loud. Against the background of new changes to the global pattern, and in the face of constantly surfacing problems in the global economy governance mechanism, the reform to this mechanism is inevitable. A "new mechanism" for governing the global economy is just round the corner.

Trade Mechanism: Barriers Wanted?

Since the advent of international trade, life has completely changed for the human race.

The "Silk Road" that links Europe with Asia not only facilitated the transport of China's precious silk products to Central Asia and European Countries, it also provided a link between the three ancient civilisations of Ancient China, Ancient India and Ancient Greece. The spices that were transported to Europe via the Mediterranean Sea not only excited the taste buds of the local people, they also made the Europeans more determined to bypass the obstacles of the Ottoman Empire and open up a new transport route for the spices.

In more recent times, the development of international trade has enabled various countries to complement one another, with stronger communication links, higher efficiency, and goods and services at lower prices, benefitting more people. The new modes of transport, such as trains, planes and high speed railways, as well as telephones, telegraphs, satellites, optical fibre cables and the Internet, all emerged to shorten the physical distances between people. This also enabled the global circulation of production essentials such as labour, capital and technology, and the global allocation of these resources. No wonder Thomas Loren Friedman exclaimed "The world is flat"!

The UK was the place where the Industrial Revolution originated. It is also a big nation for the traditional manufacturing industry. However, its domestic manufacturing industry had been accounting for a lower and lower percentage of its economy over the past three decades. Some of these manufacturing industries have even vanished from the country. Stoke was once the famous capital for ceramics, noted for their production of the expensive bone china. Now what is left is the dilapidated factory, and the bone china had long disappeared. Similar to the ceramics industry, as many as 4 million jobs were lost in UK in the past nearly 30 years. To be sure, UK's manufacturing industry has not declined. What happened was they transferred the manufacturing departments and jobs at the low end of the global value chain to emerging market economies and developing economies such as China, India and Brazil, to make the best use of their cheap labour, and at the same time secure their own core competitiveness in the high end—like knowledge and skills, so as to maintain their own competitive advantage. UK's mechanical equipment and precision food industries mushroomed in recent years, and they also led in the areas of alternative energies and low-carbon manufacturing technology.

Under these circumstances, the relationship between developed countries and developing countries is undergoing quiet change. And this, to a certain extent, is attributed to the continuously lowering hurdles against global economic development after the Second World War.

The two World Wars in the first half of the 20th century disrupted the currency and financial relationships and trade relationships that maintain the global economic development. From the Wars, countries in the world came to the awareness that economic policies based on traditional isolationism and protectionism fail to ignite the hope of the future global economy. It is only when economic cooperation is strengthened among countries that the global economy can move towards prosperity.

The WTO (formerly GATT) is in fact a multi-lateral trade mecha-

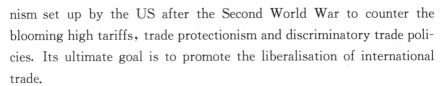

nism set up by the US after the Second World War to counter the blooming high tariffs, trade protectionism and discriminatory trade policies. Its ultimate goal is to promote the liberalisation of international trade.

As a global trade governance mechanism, the WTO (and GATT) provides for the world a platform for negotiating and resolving trade disputes. On this platform, the member countries can coordinate and resolve international trade disputes and negotiate the lowering of trade barriers, so as to reach a "win-win" and even "multi-win" situation.

China is a beneficiary of free trade, and also its loyal supporter. It rode on the opportunity created in 1998 when developed countries like US and Europe started to transfer their industries after the Asian financial crisis, and become an important base for the world's manufacturing industry. It has even been dubbed the world's factory. There are tens of thousands of manufacturing enterprises in the Pearl River Delta and Yangtze River Delta of China, fulfilling the orders from the US and European countries, and successfully creating employment for 120 million migrant workers, and the miracle of China's economic growth. In the US, as China's second largest trade partner, "Made in China" not only brought huge profits for US enterprises, it also enabled US consumers to enjoy quality products at low prices. From garments to shoes, from home electric appliances to daily necessities, "Made in China" is everywhere. Refusing to use Chinese products means lowering the standard of living. It is estimated that without these products from China, the US consumers will need to spend an extra US $ 70 billion.

At present, the international trade volume involving the global trade governance mechanism exceeds 90% of the total global trade volume. For the contracting party that comprises developed countries, their average tariff dropped from 36% in 1948 to 4.5% in the 1980s. In the same period, the contracting party that comprises developing countries saw their average tariff drop to 13%. From 1950 to 2009, the global trade of agricultural products grew at the annual average rate of 3.5%. The same rate for fuels and mineral products was 4.0%, and that for manufactured products was 7.1% (See Table 5.2).

Table 5. 2   **The Aannual Average Growth Rate of Major Global Products Trade Volume** (%)

	Agricultural products	Fuels and mineral products	Manufactured products
• 1950—1973	4. 3	7. 4	9. 8
• 1973—1990	2. 4	0. 5	5. 5
• 1990—2009	3. 6	3. 0	5. 4
• 1950—2009	3. 5	4. 0	7. 1

Source: WTO official website.

After the outbreak of the global financial crisis, protectionist trade was on the rise. At the end of May 2012, WTO, OECD and UNCTAD jointly issued their 7th Report on G20 Trade and Investment Measures. The report stated that the trade restrictions implemented since October 2008 covered 3% of global goods trading and 4% of the trading volume of G20 countries. Since the outbreak of the financial crisis, among the 802 restrictive measures, only 18% were abandoned.

Clyde Prestowitz, Director of the US Economic Strategy Research Institute, had said, in today's globalised world there are two different sets of game rules. One is the official rules of the WTO, and the other is mercantilism practised tacitly by certain countries. These countries take advantage of the ambiguities in the WTO official rules, or just turn a blind eye to these rules. These practices are called "trade protectionism" by the majority, and "defensive measures" by others.

Faced with these circumstances, the global trade governance mechanism based on the WTO needs further adjustments. The direction of adjustment should be: change the current excessively rigid dispute resolution procedures, and break the current situation where the two sets of "game rules" are practised in parallel. Then set up a clear set of standards, to enable all members of the WTO and participants in international trade to resolve disputes inside a more reasonable and fair framework, thereby realising "free trade" in the true sense of the term.

Financial Mechanism: Believe in "Big Brother"?

The international financial crisis triggered by the US subprime crisis made a huge impact on the international economic and financial system and the global economy governance structure, sending shockwaves across the global real economy. This also exposed the existing problems present in the current global financial governance mechanism.

The key cause for this problem is that the US economy is monopolistic, and the international economic operations are becoming more and more diversified. Moreover, the globalisation of the economic and financial systems is becoming more and more difficult to adapt to. Under these circumstances, it is clear that the US lacks the resources and the skill to address the risks and challenges inherent in large scale financial activities.

The current global financial governance mechanism was established after the Second World War, and is executed mainly by the International Monetary Fund (IMF) and the World Bank (WB). Like the WTO, it is led by the US and a small number of developed countries in Europe. The leading developed countries are using this mechanism as the tool to perpetuate the theories and values of free economy. At the same time, these countries are considered to be the platform for realising self interests. Since it was set up over 60 years ago, the Governor of the World Bank has always been Americans, and the managing directors of the IMF have always been Europeans. This "tradition" has never changed since these two institutions were "born" (See Table 5. 3).

Table 5. 3   **IMF Chiefs: The Managing Directors**

Tenure	Name	Nationality
➤ 6 May 1946 to 6 May 1951	Camille Gutt	Belgium
➤ 3 August 1951 to 3 Oct 1956	Lvar Rooth	Sweden
➤ 21 Nov 1956 to 5 May 1963	Per Jacobsson	Sweden
➤ 1 Sept 1963 to 1 Sept 1973	Pjerre-Paul Schweitzer	France
➤ 1 Sept 1973 to 17 June 1978	Johannes Witteveen	Netherlands
➤ 17 June 1978 to 16 Jan 1987	Jacque de Larosiere	France
➤ 16 Jan 1987 to 14 Feb 2000	Michel Camdessus	France
➤ 1 May 2000 to 4 Mar 2004	Horst Köhler	Germany
➤ 4 Mar 2004 to 4 May 2004	Anne Osborn Krueger	USA
➤ 4 May 2004 to 1 Nov 2007	Rodrigo de Rato	Spain
➤ 1 Nov 2007 to 19 May 2011	Dominique Strauss-Kahn	France
➤ 18 June 2011 to present	Christine Lagarde	France

The current IMF and WB have the problem of over-concentration of voting rights. Thus it is the manifestation of the "unfairness" of the global financial governance mechanism. The IMF members take part in the discussion and resolution of global financial issues through exercising their voting rights. From this perspective, the IMF voting right is the basis for global financial governance.

According to the rules, the IMF voting right is composed of the "basic voting right" and the "weighted voting right". The basic voting right is the fixed voting right that each member possesses. It is a reflection of the principle of sovereign fairness. This means that no matter the country is poor or rich, powerful or not, it has a basic voting right. On the other hand, the weighted voting right is similar to the mechanism of a shareholding company. The more a shareholder contributes to the company, the greater its voting quota is.

According to statistics, from 1958 to 2007, the number of fund members increased from 68 to 184, but the basic voting rights decreased from 15.6% to 2.1%. For most of the developing countries, their voting rights account for only 44% of the total voting rights. On the other hand, a small number of developed countries account for 56% of the voting right. The countries that account for the largest quota are: US 16.77%; Japan 7.85%, Germany 4.48%, France 4.30%, and UK 4.30%.

According to the IMF terms of reference, unless there are special regulations, all IMF resolutions must be passed by more than half of the voting rights, and major resolutions must be passed by over 85% of the voting rights. This resulted in a serious disparity between basic voting right and weighted voting right. The US has monopolistic dominance in IMF, and has a vetoing right in major resolutions. As a result, the sovereignty fairness principle represented by "one country one vote" gave way to the voting principle based on the "US Dollar". The over-concentration of voting rights has resulted in a small number of developed countries possessing the actual vetoing right on global financial governance resolutions. This is a departure on the global public function of correcting and supplementing market failures, and results in a serious imbalance and disorderly state in the global economy. On the one hand, it is manifested in the global economic imbalance resulting in the widening of the poverty gap. On the other hand, it is manifested in the disorderly state of the international currency system, the lack of a system arrangement for the currency exchange rate system on a global scale, and the high volatility in the currency exchange rates among reserve currencies. The disorderly flow of international capital, and the isolation of financial capital from the real economy have resulted in a self-perpetuating cycle, increasing the systemic risk of the international financial system. The reform on the international financial system and the global financial governance mechanism are set to be put into practice.

G20 is an international economic cooperation forum, and a platform for negotiating global economic governance affairs. Since its inception in Berlin on 25 September 1999, it has become an informal dialogue mechanism within the framework of the Bretton Woods System. It is composed of G8 and 11 important newly industrialised countries and European Union countries. At present, G20 has become a venue for the developing countries and developed countries to negotiate the reform of the global economic governance mechanism.

Pittsburgh in Pennsylvania was once a key industrial town in the US. It hosted the G20 Pittsburgh Summit on 24-25 September 2009. This summit reaped phenomenal progress in terms of global economic governance. The participating countries jointly resolved to strengthen mutual cooperation, to execute necessary reforms to the international financial system, especially reaching a consensus on the IMF increasing its capital and enhancing financial supervision. More specifically, this means to increase the share of emerging markets and developing countries in the IMF organisation, and to raise the voting rights of developing countries and economies in transition by at least 3% in the IMF, thereby raising the representation and right of speech in the World Bank.

The consistent effort of developing countries in reforming the global financial governance mechanism finally bore fruit in 2010. On 5 November 2010, the IMF approved the most important governance proposal since 65 years of its existence. This is also the largest share transfer proposal between emerging markets and developing countries. According to this reform proposal, as the representative of developing countries, China's share in IMF will be increased from 3.72% to

6.39%, and the voting right will be increased from 3.65% to 6.07%, overtaking Germany, France and UK, right after the US and Japan. After this round of reform, the US, Japan, the four BRIC countries (Brazil, Russia, India and China), as well as Germany, France, UK and Italy, became the top 10 economies in IMF. This reform proposal undoubtedly raised the right of speech and right of initiative of emerging economies and developing countries in the reform of the international financial system and the global economic governance mechanism.

Although there is progress in the reform of the global financial governance mechanism, yet there has not been any fundamental alteration to the original pattern of the IMF. The US still enjoys absolute vetoing right and commands a leading status. This suggests that the IMF reform will be a slow and difficult process. The reform of the global financial governance mechanism will be an important and long journey.

After the Second World War, developed countries such as the US and European countries developed the IMF, World Bank and WTO. They also coordinated trade policies, exchange rate policies, currency policies and financial policies. On top of these, they built a platform for policy coordination through the regular meeting of heads of state, in order to find a balancing point for the interests of various parties. This is the Western G7 summit meeting. (With Russia joining in 1997, G7 became G8.)

With the continued strengthening of the power of developing countries, the international macro economic policy coordination mechanism, led by the US and developed European countries, is being impacted. While it has not yet gathered strength, it still generated the effect of "moistening things silently". In particular, after the latest round of international financial crisis, the importance of the emerging economies in boosting the global economy is apparent. Under these circumstances, the developing countries are no longer a marginal force in the coordination of macro economic policies and global economic governance. They have a strong demand to build a platform for the discussion of common economic issues between developed countries and major developing countries—hence the G20 Summit. This is a platform that achieves synergy with the BRIC Summit and East Asia Summit, having a significant effect on establishing a more reasonable and just new order for international politics and economy.

The G20 is made up of G8, 11 major newly industrialised countries, and the European Union. G8 comprises the US, Japan, Germany, France, UK, Italy, Canada and Russia. The 11 major newly industrialised countries comprise China, Argentina, Australia, Brazil, India, Indonesia, Mexico, Saudi Arabia, South Africa, Korea and Turkey. The GNP of the G20 accounts for 85% of the global total. In fact, the aggregated GNP of the US, Japan, UK, Germany, France, Italy, Canada and Russia already accounts for 60% of the global GNP. Hence all along, these eight countries have been playing a leading role in the G20 establishment.

By June 2012, G20 has convened seven summits (as shown in Table 5.4). These summits have extensively discussed and reached important consensus on various issues, including tackling the financial crisis, reforming the global financial system and IMF, countering protectionism, and strengthening international financial supervision. They reflect more abundantly the demands of the newly industrialised countries and the developing countries, and have great significance in, profound influences on, the establishment of a more reasonable and just new order for international politics and economy, and setting up a global economic governance mechanism that reflects the needs of the times more faithfully.

Table 5.4   **The Various G20 Summits**

	Time and Place	Content
First Summit	15 November 2008 Washington, USA	The summit discussed global financial and economic issues. A declaration was issued, stressing that in the face of challenges in the global economy and international financial markets, the participating countries should strengthen cooperation and resume the global growth, and realise the necessary reforms in the global financial system. The summit reaped positive results in strengthening the synergy in the international community, in consolidating efforts to tackle the financial crisis and to support economic growth in order to devise a plan for reforming the financial and economic system. The summit also called for reforming the global financial system to prevent similar crises from recurring.

Cont.

	Time and Place	Content
Second Summit	1 – 4 April 2009 UK	A number of agreements were made among participating heads of state regarding a global joint effort in tackling the financial economic crisis, such as increasing the capital of IMF and strengthening financial supervision. The declaration after the summit reiterated the determination to counter protectionism. The participating heads of state unanimously agreed to include hedge funds into the scope of financial supervision.
Third Summit	24 – 25 September 2009 Pittsburgh, USA	The main agenda of the summit included driving the recovery of the global economy and reforming the international financial system. One of the most important achievements of the summit was the reform of the governance structure of the IMF. According to the summit's resolution, developed countries must transfer some of the quota to developing countries, and the quota for developed countries was raised from 43% to 48%. According to the "Declaration of the Leaders" issued at the summit the G20 heads of state agreed to increase the shift for emerging markets and developing countries in IMF by at least 5%, and to increase the voting rights of developing countries and economies in transition by at least 3%. The G20 will become the "major forum for international economic cooperation", and the G20 Summit will become a regular annual event starting in 2011.
Fourth Summit	26 – 27 June 2010 Toronto, Canada	The Toronto Summit struck the keynote for growth, and honoured the major agenda of "strong, sustainable and balanced growth framework", and of financial supervision. The heads of state also raised specific schedules for developed countries to cut their financial deficits, to reform the governance of international financial institutions, and to counter protectionism. They stressed that the top priority of G20 countries was to ensure and strengthen economic recovery. The summit issued the "G20 Toronto Summit Declaration", stressing the need to take the next step and drive the global economy into strong, sustainable and balanced growth.

Cont.

	Time and Place	Content
Fifth Summit	11 - 12 November 2010 Seoul, Korea	The main agenda was exchange rate, global financial safety net, international financial structure reform, and development. Among the four major agenda items, the one that people were most concerned about was the follow-up developments of an agreement on the exchange rate dispute and the reform for the shift of IMF quota shares reached by the G20 finance ministers and central bank governors.
Sixth Summit	3 November 2011 Cannes, France	Discussed the global economy situation, "strong, sustainable and peaceful framework", important and stringent international economic and financial issues, international currency system reform, prices of bulk commodity, global governance, trade, development and financial supervision. The participating members reiterated the synergistic commitments aimed to resurrect the economy, to create jobs, to ensure financial stability, to drive social tolerance, and to make sure that globalisation meets the demands for humankind. In "The Cannes Action Plan for Growth and Jobs" passed at the summit, the G20 members promised to tackle within a short period the fragility of the economy, to resume financial stability, and on the medium term to strengthen the foundation for economic growth. All the G20 members will further drive the structural reform, explore potentials for growth, facilitate employment, strengthen the stability of the international financial system, and advocate freedom of trade and investment. The Cannes Summit reached three consensus items: (1) To ensure that the IMF has adequate resources to carry out its plan, and will go for new capital increase on the basis of common knowledge. (2) To take all measures to promote economic growth. (3) To stress that the social security system is also a favourable factor in promoting economic growth. The G20 members, especially the emerging market countries, promised to set up and perfect the social security system.

Cont.

	Time and Place	Content
Seventh Summit	18 – 19 June 2012 Los Cabos, Mexico	The focuses of discussion at the summit included the global economic situation, strengthening the international financial system, and the issues of development, trade and employment. The participating heads of state unanimously agreed that the international community should be well-coordinated in driving the strong, sustainable and balanced development of the global economy. The G20 approved the "Los Cabos Growth and Jobs Action Plan" in order to realise economic growth, to maintain financial stability, and to create employment opportunities.

The new changes to the global economic pattern requires that corresponding changes be made to the original coordinating mechanism of the global macro economic policies. The developing countries, especially the emerging industrialised economies, advocate the continued implementation of the multi-lateral mechanism of G20 and the United Nations etc. on the one hand, and on the other hand, it emphasises that there should be coordination and governance among developing countries, and between developing countries and developed countries. It also advocates enhancing the right of speech and representation of developing countries, and setting up a more just international financial framework and global economy governance framework to ensure the long-term, sustainable, steady and healthy development of the global economy.

Gaming in Governance: "Losses" and "Gains" of China and the US

A decade passes in one split second. While the bells of the new century are still reverberating, what we see in front of us are the ruins of the global financial tsunami. As the different countries are still under the threat of the residual shockwaves, they face the new adjustments to the global economic pattern.

In this adjustment, US and China are particularly in the limelight.

One is a rising new star in economic development, the other is a robust economic power. The gaming and balance between these two countries are what a lot of people are watching with expectation and interest.

US: Still the "Locomotive"

2012 saw an obvious slowdown in the pace of economic recovery in the US. There are four reasons:

First, the leverage used by the US Government to stimulate the economy has almost been used up, and QE3 is still waiting to be launched. Hence we can see that the US Government is powerless in its implementation of economy-stimulating policies. Moreover, the economic measures already implemented—such as the export doubling strategy, the policy to create jobs, and the policy to support US enterprises, have not been effective.

Second, the US domestic unemployment has been steadily on the rise, and so is the rate of saving. This restrained the spending desire of the US citizens, and so consumption clearly fails to have a pulling effect on economic growth.

Third, the US property market is still gloomy, and this dampens the recovery of the US manufacturing industry, and slows down the overall growth rate of the US economy.

Fourth, the European debt crisis continues to spread. This not only amplified the turmoil of the international financial market, but also seriously undermined the confidence of the investors, sending shockwaves across the US stock market.

At present, the factors that caused the slowdown of the US economic growth are clearly perpetuating. In the short run, it is clear that the periodic recovery of the US economy will not reverse, but the pace of economic growth is expected to be very limited. To alter this situation, the US Federal Reserves announced that in the coming two years the relaxation of monetary policy will be maintained. This once again proves one thing—that is, the US Government will have difficulty finding more effective policy tools to stimulate economic development.

As the US Government budget and the new proposals to stimulate the economy repeatedly failed, the current US President Barack Obama has made a proposal to the Congress to levy heavier tax on the rich, in order to make sure that the rich Americans with an annual income of over US$1 million pay tax at a rate not lower than the middle income group. He even called this proposal the "Buffett Tax".

The US economy is facing its own structural problems and debt issues. Although a lot of people expect the US economy to continue to slip, there is no doubt that the US is still the "locomotive" of the global economy. In 2011, China accounted for 9.98% of the global economy. Japan accounted for 8.36%, Germany 5.18%, UK 3.54%, and the US 21.51%. Although the US share in the global economy declined from 24.6% in 2009, yet this share is still far larger than other countries. There is a saying that goes, "When the US sneezes, the whole world catches a cold." This is a vivid way to describe the status of the US economy in the global economy. Five years ago, when the "subprime crisis" just started, the situation was just that several hundreds of thousands of US families failed to repay their mortgage, but finally it dragged the global economy to the abyss of recession. This shows how the vicissitudes of the US can have a global impact.

We had mentioned earlier that there are 7 billion people in the world. China and India account for 2.5 billion, but they spend less than US$6,000 billion (China has 1.3 billion people, and they spend more than US$3,000 billion). Although the US has only 300 million people, their total spending reached US$11,000 billion. So it is evident that the US is the engine of global economic growth. Spending is the short-term driving force for global economic growth, and production and innovation are the basic force that drives global economic growth.

The most outstanding feature of the US innovation system is that the country makes enterprises the core part of technology innovation and industrialisation. Nike, a world renowned manufacturer of sports equipment, has its headquarters in Oregon, USA. In the 1990s, Nike's annual sales reached over US$10 billion, making it a leading world class enterprise. The reason for Nike's popularity is to a large extent their continued dertermination to innovate. With their spirit of innovation, Nike's designers not only designed Nike's "air" and "shox" air-cushioned sports shoes, inspired by distance runners from Africa who run barefooted, they also designed the "Free" series of shoes using two wide leather belts to replace the traditional shoe laces. In fact, Nike not only focuses on product innovation, they also focus on innovation of their operating strategies. They adopt a virtual strategy that takes advantage of external forces. This actually is the reality of their virtual production. Nike does not invest in building a production site, and they do not assemble a production line. Through integrating external resources, they outsource all their orders to other factories for processing, in order to gain low cost advantage in competing with other brands.

After the global financial crisis, different countries have devised different innovation strategies with different focuses. The US has set up six strategic industries to boost economic development, with their focus on new energy sources. Europe's innovative strategy focuses on life sciences, and the innovative focus of Asia Pacific's emerging market economies is on information industry. While the new round of demands and innovations (new driving forces) of the global economy is still unclear, it is nevertheless evident that future innovation will still depend on the US, and new energy sources are likely to be the area to have the first breakthroughs, and also the most promising direction. It is very likely that the US will produce the inventions that can drive the world economy, and China will be the place where mass production takes place.

Barack Obama took over the US Administration at a time of crisis. In the process of overcoming economic crises, the Obama Government gave strong support to the development of new energy industries. After his ascension to power, he drastically changed the energy policy of the Bush Administration—he declared that in the coming decade his administration would invest US$150 billion to support the research on alternative energies to reduce the emission of carbon dioxide by 5 billion tons. He also promised to approve new legislation to reduce 80% of the US greenhouse gas emissions by 2050 compared with 1990. He also lowered the tax on energy-saving cars to encourage consumers to buy them. Analysis shows that using the latest technologies, the US can save half of the consumption of petroleum and natural gas, and three quarters of the electricity. New energy strategies have a special significance for the US at this time.

In 2011, the US dependency on petroleum imports was 66% (China was 56.5%). If there is a breakthrough in the new energy strategy, the first benefit will be that the US will be less dependent on the import of petroleum. The Obama Government plans to invest US＄150 billion in the coming 10 years in the production of clean energy and renewable energy sources, and proposed that the reduction in the consumption of petroleum in the next 10 years will exceed the total import at present from the Middle East and Venezuela. Secondly, the important breakthroughs in new energies and environmental protection technologies in the US will effectively enhance the international competitiveness of US industries, and drive a new round of economic growth in the country. More importantly, the US has initiated inter-industry new technology revolution and new industry revolution driven by new energies. The purpose of this initiative is to take the lead in mastering the key technologies in energy and environment, thereby commanding a controlling status in the global value chain of the new energy industries. The effect of this will be that other countries will have to depend on the US for the technologies, thus guaranteeing the leadership of the US in the new round of global economic development.

Although the US is in a difficult situation, yet in the face of the lingering repercussions of the international financial crisis, and the growing strength of the emerging market economies who demand a reform in global governance, the country is determined to devise a new set of game rules for its own benefit.

1. First, The US Wants to Maintain its Leadership in the International Financial System

With the US economy emerging from the abyss of its economic periodic cycle, the US has entered its "economic age of banknote printing". By printing large amounts of banknotes, the US Dollar has depreciated. This not only diluted the country's huge debt liabilities, it also compensated for its international trade deficits, exporting inflation to the world. There is also a hidden agenda in this—to maintain the US-centric international currency system and the US's global currency status.

The oil crisis in the 1970s caused the liquidity panic in the world. The result was that the various countries were forced to abandon the gold-based currency system and set up the international currency system using the US Dollar as the international standard currency. In doing so, the US gained a special authority that transcends other countries. This is tantamount to having the right to issue currency without restraints. When the subprime crisis first broke out in the US in 2007, the total debt in the US amounted to only US$ 8,900 billion, and the debt ratio was 65%. In 2011, however, the US's total debt already exceeded US$ 14,000 billion, with the debt ratio approaching 100%.

We need to point out that the volume of currency issue in the US is directly related to the government debt issued by the US Treasury. The US Federal Reserve is responsible for issuing currency, while the US Treasury is responsible for issuing government debt. The US Federal Reserve uses its own issued currency (US Dollars) to buy the government debt of the US Federal Government, and the US Treasury uses the government debt as security to arrange financing with the US Federal Reserve to fund its expenditure. In other words, the basis for the US Federal Reserve to invest in basic currency is US government debt. Therefore, the US over-issuing national debt means the US Dollar is over-invested. And the US Dollar, as an international savings currency, can be over-invested under a condition of no restraint. This will inevitably result in a liquidity flood in the world. Then what follows is a general price rise in global bulk commodities and general goods, resulting in a global increase in production costs and a decline in the standard of living. To avoid the impact of liquidity, most countries will approve the floating exchange rate to avert risk, and high volatility in exchange rate will definitely have a negative impact on international trade.

In this process, the US approved the over-issue of the US Dollar and gained the "seigniorage" on the one hand, and on the other hand, the expansion-based currency policy has also stimulated a growing demand for imports, at the expense of the welfare of the citizens of other countries, to support the rise in the welfare of US citizens (See Figure 5. 1).

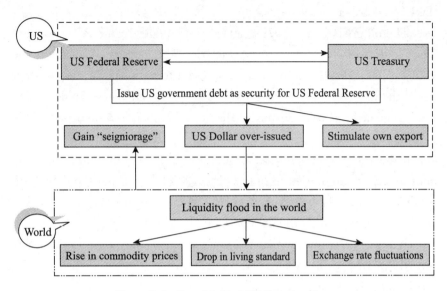

Figure 5.1 Secret behind US Currency Issue

Also out of state interest considerations, the US is striving to maintain its own status in the international financial system. In December 2010, the International Monetary Fund (IMF) Executive Board approved the governance and quota reform proposal, with resolutions including transferring about 6% of the quota to vibrant emerging industrialised markets and developing countries ("quota reform proposal"). It was also decided that the Executive Board will be revamped. The European countries will give up two seats to emerging markets and developing countries, to create a more representative, elected Executive Board ("Executive Board Reform Proposal"). These two proposals are planned for completion by the annual meetings of the World Bank and the IMF in October 2012. Although this reform is not the entire reform of the fund organisation governance structure, it is also an important measure for the organisation to implement reforms.

However, the implementation of this reform proposal leaves much to be desired. Up to 12 June 2012, the number of member countries in the fund organisation that approved this quota reform proposal reached 107, but these countries account for only 66.84% of the membership in IMF. According to the regulations, the quota reform proposal needs to be approved by over 70% of the member countries before it can take effect. 80 member countries approved the Executive Board's reform proposal—these countries' voting rights account for 55.06% of the total voting rights of IMF. According to the regulations, the Executive Board reform proposals need to have 85% of the total voting rights from member countries to take effect. (IMF has the regulation that major decisions need to have 85% of the total voting rights to take effect.) And the US possesses over 16% of the voting rights. This means that the US holds the vetoing right on major reform decisions.

The basic viewpoint of the US in improving the global financial governance mechanism is: it agrees to reform, but wants to maintain and consolidate its own core leadership status in this mechanism. The US is of the view that the future US Dollar will be issued by the US, and all the countries of the world should take responsibility and give support so that the US currency will become the public asset of the world. This is the most ideal system.

2. Implement Trade Protectionism, and Revive the Domestic Economy

Following this round of international financial crisis, "returning to the manufacturing industry" has become the common concern for the political, academic and enterprise circles. This is the conclusion drawn by various sectors in the US after reflecting on the domestic industry structure and economic development mode.

The US Government hopes to use "returning to the manufacturing industry" as a breakthrough point to revitalise the domestic economy. Through "returning to the manufacturing industry", the US can secure a strategic foothold in the new round of science and technology competition and industry competition on the one hand, and on the other hand, lead the domestic manufacturers to expand re-production. This can improve the employment rate which has always been low in the US, and at the same time break through the constraint of "despite economic growth there is no employment growth", resulting from the upgrade of industry structure. This will help to alleviate the social contradictions aggravated by domestic economic downturn and low employment rate.

Along the line of "returning to the manufacturing industry" and adjusting the industry structure, the US Government started a new round of trade protectionism in 2009.

In early 2009, the US—then in a state of economic recession—launched a US $ 819 billion economy boosting plan, with the rule that the rescue funds can only be used "to buy US goods". This was the "prelude" to the US implementation of trade protectionism.

In 2010, the US further strengthened its management system on imported goods. The "Food Safety Modernization Act" signed by the US President raised the demands for imported products—imported goods must have undergone the total control of food safety—so as to raise the threshold for food import. At the same time, the US Government also raised the demands for energy consumption standards and labeling, including requiring all TV sets and electric lights to have energy consumption labels. Moreover, the implementation of the US foreign trade laws (including anti-dumping and countervailing investigation) signified a more serious and stringent attitude.

The target of this round of trade protectionism is China, which is the source country for US's greatest foreign trade deficit. As a result, the China-US trade friction grew more heated. What is at play behind this, is not just the apparent economic factors, but also the political interest background that 2012 is an election year. Apart from the change of president, the congressmen and one third of the senators will be changed in 2012. Hence from the White House to the Congress, everybody is trying to set up an image of fighting for public interest. In the eyes of some US politicians in the US, if you raise the flag of trade protectionism, you stand a good chance of winning the support of voters.

3. Try to Lead a New Mode of Global Trade

Apart from implementing trade protectionism policies, the US has also tried to lead a new mode of global trade by expanding its presence in the Asia Pacific trade map, thus isolating China. The Trans-Pacific Strategic Economic Partnership (TPP) is actually a point of breakthrough.

In 1994, Asia-Pacific Economic Cooperation (APEC) leaders held a conference at Bogor to explore the possibility of implementing free trade and investment. This affirmed the objective of setting up the "Free Trade Area of the Asia Pacific" (FTAAP). In 2002, the member countries of Chile, New Zealand and Singapore—three APEC member countries—started the TPP talks. This was a solid step to take in reaching the FTAAP goals.

In 2008, the US joined the TPP talks, giving new meaning to the region's little trade framework. In 2011, US Secretary of State Hilary Clinton published in the magazine *Foreign Policy* an article titled "The US's Pacific Century". This fully shows that the US has already shifted its foreign policy and strategic focus towards the Asia Pacific, and TPP has become an integrated component.

The core thinking in the US developing TPP is to exclude China, and to break through the traditional Free Trade Agreement by reaching an integrated free trade agreement that includes all goods and services. By mid-November 2011, a total of 10 countries had taken part in the TPP talks. These countries include the US, Brunei, Chile, New Zealand, Singapore, Australia, Peru, Vietnam, Malaysia and Japan. The total production of this free trade zone has reached one-third of the global total. The US also strives to expand the TPP membership to 12 countries. If this plan succeeds, then the TPP will cover a market of 800 million people, accounting for about 40% of the global economy. This is even larger than the total of 27 countries in the European Union.

There are three core issues within the TPP framework. First, to raise human rights and labour standards. Second, to raise the standards for environmental protection. Third, to raise the protective standards of intellectual rights. These standards are consistent with OECD standards. In other words, these are the standards of the developed countries. In these standards, the US has an advantage in every sense of the word. The US wants to take advantage of TPP to create a high-standard trade agreement that is applicable not only to the Asia Pacific region in the future, but also to the world. If TPP succeeds, it will be tantamount to the US creating the second WTO, setting new game rules for the global economy.

It is well known that the FTAAP includes the ASEAN 10 + 3,

ASEAN 10＋6, and APEC. Apart from APEC, the other two FTAs do not have US representation. TPP can be seen as one of the means for the US-led alliance to exert global balance on China. Although President Obama has reiterated many times that suppressing the rise of China is not a state policy for US, yet judging from the US actively joining and driving the TPP talks, it is clear that the global strategy of the US has changed from "cooperating with China" to "counter-balancing China".

In September 2005, Fareed Zakaria, the then editor-in-chief of *Newsweek* of the US, published an article titled "China Now?". The article analysed the psychological attitude of the "Americans" towards the "Rise of China": "China has dealt a heavy blow to the self-confidence of the Americans. " The Americans like good things, but in reality what attracts their eyeballs is big things. For instance, the Grand Canyon, the Californian Red Fir, the grand central processing unit, Disney World, General Motors, the US Army, GE, double burgers (plus yogurt), and the venti cup of Starbucks.

Americans love scale, especially mega scale. And China is a country that makes the US small. China has a population of 1. 3 billion (four times that of the US). China is very large, and was very poor. But all these are changing. The mega scale that was so attractive in the past is now a source of anxiety. Moreover, the Americans are not sure if the "China threat" will actually materialise.

In the long term, the establishment of a just, reasonable and all-win order for the global economy has been a historical necessity. In the short term, US leadership in the global economy is still secure—their leading status in the global economic governance mechanism is still unshakable. This is because the US has the world top economic strength, technological strength, innovative strength, military strength and powerful national soft skills to support its supremacy. Hence, for a rather long period into the future, the existing global economic governance mechanism is still irreplaceable. The restructuring and adjustments to the US economic structure will have profound repercussions on the reform of the global industry pattern and the global economic governance mechanism.

China: Willing to Be a "Voltage Stabiliser"

As a "star of economic growth", China is enjoying a rising status in the global economy.

On the one hand, China's status as the "world factory" is becoming more and more robust. In 2010, China's share in the global production of raw steel, cement, electrolytic aluminium, refined copper and coal accounts for 44. 3%, 60%, 65%, 24% and 45% respectively. Its production of chemical fertilisers, plastics, chemical fibres and glass accounts for 35%, 20%, 42. 6% and 50% respectively of the global total volume. China's production of cars, ships and engineering machines accounts for 25%, 41. 9% and 43% respectively of the global total volume, and its production of computers, colour TV sets, refrigerators, air-conditioners, mobile phones and digital cameras commands a share of 68%, 50%, 65%, 80%, 70% and 65% respectively of the global total volume.

On the other hand, with its economic strength growing, China is starting to participate more deeply in the global economic governance mechanism, striving to bring it to perfection, in order to set up a new order for the global economy that is more reasonable and just.

On the issue of global economic governance, China and the US take different approaches. The US is attempting to re-create a new set of game rules for the global economy in order to lead in the global economic governance structure and resume or mend the original economic growth pattern led by the locomotive of US financial innovation. Meanwhile, China acts from the standpoint of the wider context of developing countries and newly industrialised economies. It is against using regional free trade rules to counter or replace the multi-lateral talks of the WTO, and it is committed to setting up a global economic governance mechanism that can benefit more countries and more people.

The "game" between China and the US has begun. Judging from the current state of affairs, the best result of this game is the achievement of inclusive growth in the global context.

China's accession into the WTO in 2001 was a significant milestone for China's in-depth participation and globalisation. In 2011, China's goods trading volume has risen from global sixth to global second, and global first in terms of export volume. Meanwhile, its accumulative total of imports reached US $ 7,500 billion, and the direct investments from overseas reached US $ 759.5 billion accumulatively, commanding top position among developing countries. On the other hand, its foreign direct investments are increasing at a rate of 40% annually, reaching US $ 68.8 billion in 2010, ranking fifth in the world. Every year, China imports an average of US $ 750 billion of goods, creating a large number of jobs and investment opportunities. Meanwhile, the foreign investors in China reap a total repatriation of profit of US $ 261.7 billion accumulatively, with an annual growth of 30%.

Accompanying the footsteps of participation in globalisation, China has grown a batch of multinational enterprises with global impact. Li Shufu's Geely Automobile Holdings acquired Volvo, and Liu Chuanzhi's Lenovo Group integrated the IBM personal computers. Ren Zhengfei's Huawei Techologies has set up branches in different parts of the world. The Industrial and Commercial Bank of China (ICBC) has acquired 20% of the largest bank of South Africa—Standard Bank of South Africa. Zoomlion Heavy Industry has acquired 100% of the equity of CIFA of Italy to become the world's largest manufacturer of cement machinery...

Up to the end of 2008, China has over 8,500 domestic investors setting up 12,000 foreign direct investment enterprises in 174 countries (or territories) in the world, with an accumulated volume of direct investments of US $ 183.97 billion, and with the total assets of overseas enterprises amounting to over US $ 1,000 billion. The pace of Chinese enterprises "going out" has been difficult but steadfast. Different from the previous investments in the low end international division of labour processes in overseas infrastructure and manufacturing industries, Chinese entrepreneurs are now more inclined to invest in higher value-added areas such as equipment manufacturing, electronic information, finance and new energies, taking an active part in the international division of labour in the new pattern of global economy.

In its development process in foreign trade and foreign investment, China has been active in reforming and perfecting the international currency system and bulk commodities pricing mechanism, and in promoting economic globalisation and regional economic unification. China proactively took up its responsibilities in the global economy that matched its current situation—to support the WTO's Doha Round of World Trade Talks, to take part in the coordination of international macro economic policies, and to take part in the setting up of the global economic governance mechanisms such as G20.

1. Applying China's Own Effort in Promoting the Liberalisation of International Trade

Since the accession into the WTO, the Chinese Government has actively fulfilled its original promises. It has continuously expanded its market entry certification in the agricultural, manufacturing and service industries. It has continuously lowered its tariffs for imports, abandoned all the import quotas that do not comply with the WTO regulations, abandoned non-tariff measures such as permits, opened up all foreign trade operating rights, and drastically lowered the threshold for the entry of foreign capital.

From 2001 to 2011, China's total tariff level was reduced from 15.3% to 9.8%, reaching and even exceeding the requirement of WTO for developing countries. Patrick Messerlin, Director of the Global Economy Unit of the Institut d' Etudes Politiques de Paris, is of the view that China has accepted the most stringent conditions for the sake of the accession into the WTO.

Over the past decade, China has 100 service departments for trade liberalisation—approaching the level of developed countries. Take Shanghai as an example. The total assets of the city's foreign banks increased fourfold from under RMB 200 billion in 2001 (when it entered into the WTO) to RMB 1,000 billion at the end of October 2011.

Shanghai's foreign banks now include HSBC, Bank of East Asia, Standard Chartered Bank, Citibank and Bank of Tokyo-Mitsubishi—all of which have individual assets exceeding RMB 100 billion. HSBC alone has over RMB 270 billion in total assets.

To ensure that it fulfills the pledge made when China entered into the WTO, the Chinese Government has been cleaning up on a large scale the related laws and regulations. Within 10 years, the Chinese Government has cleaned up over 2,300 laws and regulations and department regulations, and the local governments have cleaned up over 190,000 local policies as well as rules and regulations.

China's imports in the first decade of its accession into the WTO have created for its trade partners an equivalent of 14 million jobs. Meanwhile, the foreign investors in China have reaped an accumulated profit of US\$262 billion, with an annual growth of 30%. China's foreign investmententerprises have employed nearly 800,000 local staff, and every year they pay local taxes in excess of US\$10 billion. According to a research by US Goldman Sachs, from 2000 to 2009, China's accrued contribution to the global economy exceeded 20%, higher than the US. In 2009, China's imports grew by 2.8%, and became the only country with an increase in imports among the major economies. When the global trade volume decreased by 12.9%, China's imports still exceeded US\$1,000 billion and the country became the world's second largest importing country, making significant contribution to global economic recovery.

In the past, WTO had only one decision-making mechanism—the "four-side" mechanism formed by the US, Japan, the European Union and Canada. After China's accession, WTO formed a "seven-side" decision-making mechanism comprising China, India, the US, Brazil, European Union, Japan, and Australia. The emerging market economies and developing countries have entered the core management that leads talks, and their collective bargaining power has been drastically increased. China played a constructive role in the WTO's Doha Round of World Trade Talks. It submitted over 100 proposals, took the initiative to coordinate the standpoints of different parties, and actively carried out lobbying in order to create a more open and fair environment for international trade.

On the one hand, China actively took part in building a multi-lateral trade mechanism. On the other hand, it attached great importance to promote bilateral and regional economic and trade cooperation.

In the decade after accession into the WTO, China has become the most important and steadiest trade partner of Arabic countries. In 2010, bilateral trades reached US $ 149. 43 billion. China invested in Arabic countries an accumulated US $ 15 billion, and the Arabic countries invested accumulatively over US $ 2. 58 billion in China. Chinese enterprises have accumulatively implemented US $ 92. 5 billion worth of infrastructural facilities in Arabic countries.

In the decade after the accession into the WTO, China became the second largest trade partner for Latin America—a great leap from its previous status as a marginal trade partner. Its median trade volume increased from under US $ 15 billion at the start of the 21st century to US $ 183 billion in 2010, with an average annual growth of 28. 4%. China's rapid economic growth has brought to Latin America huge opportunities for trade prosperity. For many Latin American countries, developing trade relations with China have freed them from the previous situation where they had to rely solely on the US and European markets. Osvaldo Rosales, Director of International Trade and Integration Division of the ECLAC (Economic Commission for Latin America and the Caribbean) of United Nations, stated frankly that in this round of international financial crisis, the Latin American countries were the first to experience economic recovery, and this to a certain extent could be attributed to the support rendered by the Asian market in which China is a major player.

In Asia, China is currently the largest trade partner of Japan, Korea, North Korea, Mongolia, India and Vietnam etc. The China-ASEAN Free Trade Agreement Zone has effectively facilitated the process of unification of the Asian economy. Up to the end of 2011, China has become ASEAN's largest trade partner. In 2011, the volume of trade between China and ASEAN set a new record, reaching US $ 362. 33 billion, an increase of 24% over the same period in the previous year. Indeed, China has become the booster for ASEAN's economic development. As the world's manufacturing base, China needs many raw materials and spare parts from ASEAN countries. A lot of Southeast Asia's minerals, raw materials and spare parts are transported to China for assembly into products that are exported to Western countries such as the US. Among the products exported from ASEAN to China, the biggest category is electrical and mechanical products that have higher added values. In 2010, these products amounted to US $ 82. 94 billion, an increase of 39. 4% over the previous year, and accounted for 53. 7% of ASEAN's total exports to China. China's purchase of these products created more job opportunities for ASEAN countries.

The decade after China's accession into the WTO was also the decade that saw a dramatic growth in trade between China and Europe. To date, the European Union has been China's biggest trade partner, the biggest export market and the second biggest import market. For many years, China has been the European Union's second largest trade partner and the biggest source of imports. In 2009, China overtook Russia as the European Union's third largest export market. In the same year, the European Union became China's third largest source of foreign capital. At the end of 2010, there were 1,688 foreign investment enterprises in China from 27 European Union countries, operating 32, 944 investment projects, with the total investment amounting to a total of US $ 74. 56 billion. At the same time, Chinese enterprises have started to invest in Europe. In 2008, the head office of the COSCO Group won a tender for the franchise of a container port in Piraeus, Greece, for 35 years. In 2010, Geely Holding Group spent US $ 1. 8 billion to acquire 100% of the equity of Volvo of Sweden, becoming a classic case study in China's investment in Europe.

2. Facilitating the Reform of the International Financial System

After the international financial crisis, the recovery of the global economy continued. However, with interwining issues such as the excessive global liquidity and the imperfections of the international currency system, the road to recovery was hazardous.

To prevent the high volatility in exchange rates and the prices of bulk purchases and energy, and to ensure the sustained development of global trade and the orderly flow of capital, the reform of the international financial system is now imperative.

After the global financial crisis, the Chinese Government expedited the reform on the international financial system. In 2009, the G20 Summit in London signified the end of the old order of the global economy, and the start of a new order. The first crisis in the 21st century showed once again that the history of the G7 controlling the global economic affairs is no longer sustainable. The G20 London Summit was therefore an exploration on a global scale of how to resolve this crisis. Prior to this Summit, People's Bank of China Governor Zhou Xiaochuan admitted that it was necessary to create an international reserve currency that is not pegged to any sovereign nation and can maintain stability over the long term, in order to solve the long series of problems in the existing international currency system that were exposed during the financial crisis. To a certain extent, Zhou Xiaochuan's attitude represented the view of the Chinese Government.

Regarding the reform of the international financial system, the Chinese Government on the one hand stressed the need to use the IMF quota and voting rights as the breakthrough point to reform the existing international financial system and to boost the representation of developing countries and their right of speech. On the other hand, the Chinese Government advocates the basic function of the IMF, World Bank and G20 as the platform for global economic governance. The Chinese Government also used this as a prerequisite for actively exploring effective mechanisms and ways to step up the supervision and control over the issue of US Dollars, and at the same time set up an international reserve currency system that is stable, orderly, and adjustable in its total amount.

At the end of 2010, the IMF Board of Governors passed a reform proposal on governance and quota reform. If this proposal takes effect, it will in real terms boost the representation of emerging market economies and developing countries in IMF. This will be a significant milestone in the reform of the global financial governance mechanism.

Apart from this, China also approved a RMB swapping agreement with other economies, to facilitate the reform of the international reserve currency system. In 2000, 10 ASEAN countries and the 3 countries of China, Japan and Korea passed the "Chiang Mai Initiative" to set up a regional currency swapping network. Since then, and up to March 2012, China has set up currency swapping relationships with 19 economies including New Zealand, Singapore, Iceland, Argentina, Indonesia, Belarus, Malaysia, Hong Kong of China and Korea. The accumulated amount reached RMB 1,600 billion.

The currency swapping agreements that China has signed with other economies, under the disorderly situation of the current international currency system, has built a regional currency swapping network, and manifested China's responsibility as a big nation, as well as its determination and contribution in maintaining the stability of the regional currencies. At the same time, since June 2012, China and Japan have been carrying out currency transactions. This to a certain extent has reduced the reliance on the US Dollar. While averting the risk of US Dollar depreciation, this is also conducive to maintaining the stability of the international financial market.

3. Promoting the Establishment of a New Order for the International Economy That Is More Just and Reasonable

In 2000, the heads of state and heads of government of over 150 countries gathered in New York to attend the United Nations Millennium Summit at the headquarters of the United Nations. The theme of the summit was "The Role of the United Nations at the Turn of the 21st Century". Then United Nations Secretary-General Kofi Atta Annan urged all countries to take action to strive to free 1 billion people from poverty. Unfortunately, the pledges made at the Millennium Summit have not been fulfilled in the first decade. Rather, the imbalance in economic development among different countries worsened, and the south-north gap widened. In 1990, the per capita average income of the top income countries was 64 times that of the lowest income countries. In 2009, this figure increased to 75 times.

Then the binary structure in the developing world took shape. In the first decade of the 21st century, there appeared among the developing countries, the middle income countries and the low income countries, and on the lowest rung, the poorest countries saw the polarisation of different communities within the country. In 1990, the average GDP of middle-low income countries was 23. 6 times that of low income countries. In 2009, this difference widened to 39. 4 times.

After the Millennium Summit, China has all along been honouring its pledge by building partnerships for a new type of global development that is more equal and more balanced, and also by strengthening south-north dialogue and south-south cooperation. In the past nearly a decade, China's accumulated assistance funds provided to other countries a-mounted to over RMB 170 billion. China has exempted 50 heavily-indebted and least developed countries from debts due amounting to nearly RMB 30 billion. China has also pledged to grant zero tariff concessions to 97% of the products of the least developed countries with diplomatic ties with China. It has also provided training to over 60,000 people from 173 developing countries and 13 regional international organisations, with an aim to enable these countries to carry out autonomous development.

China is also very concerned about setting up the south-south cooperation mechanism. The Forum on China-Africa Cooperation advocated by China is such a collective dialogue mechanism. Since the first ministerial conference of the Forum on China-Africa Cooperation was held in Beijing in 2000, the Forum has gone a long way, with five ministerial conferences held. At present, there are already 48 member countries. These member countries have started cooperative projects in trade, investment, finance, agriculture, resources, travel, education, science, culture, health and social welfare. As the largest developing country in the world, China has responded positively to the call of the UN Millennium Summit to fulfill international obligations, setting its eyes on the future, and working towards eliminating the south-north imbalance.

Future: Realising "Mutual Sharing"

In the age of economic globalisation, there are countless intertwining economic relationships among different countries in the world. "you are among us and we are among you".

Before the onset of the global financial crisis, the values of freedom and market were prevalent in the global context. But after the crisis, many governments have re-introduced the economic intervention policy on a large scale. During the post-crisis period, in the process of recovery of the global economy, competition between enterprises will continue to give way to the gaming and competing among governments.

The governments of developed countries in the US and Europe have raised the strategy of "re-industrialisation", to address the problems of the declining importance of industry, and the falling competitiveness of certain industries in the global market.

The aims of these measures were to encourage industry investments to "return" to the country, and to boost the rapid growth of the domestic manufacturing industry. In 2009, the Obama Government in the US proposed to re-vitalise the domestic manufacturing industry, leading the US to an economic development mode driven by exports. In the same year, the German Government proposed the "initiation of a new round of industrialisation", to resurrect the traditional manufacturing industry.

In the face of the adjustments in development strategy among Western countries, the economic future is worrying for the developing countries at the lower end of the international industrial division of labour chain—countries who rely on the market of the developed countries. Fredrik Erixon, Director of the European Centre for International Political Economy, pointed out that since the onset of the international financial crisis in 2008, there were deep changes in the trade relationship between China and Europe. China's light industry exports to the European Union dropped drastically. Europe is strengthening its "trade defence" to help their enterprises compete with their rivals in China.

Under these circumstances, the Chinese Government made a timely shift in its national economic development strategy. It proposed making a change to the mode of foreign trade growth, riding on a new round of international industry transformation and upgrading of the processing trade, repositioning itself in the division of labour in the global value chain.

Jiangsu Province accounts for about half of China's processing trade volume, and has long been called the "wind vane of foreign trade". Jiangsu's competitive advantage, based on low-cost, outsource-type and lower-end division of labour, is now draining out. On the one hand, it is due to the slowdown of the foreign demand market, shrinking of the foreign demand level, increasing international competition and escalating trade friction. On the other hand, it is also due to the rising costs of the labour force and raw materials. Up to the first half of 2012, Jiangsu Province has experienced a "recession type deficit" for four to five years. In the first six months of 2012, the Province's import-export growth rate was 6.6% lower than the national average, and its import growth rate was under 5.1%, lower than the five comparable coastal provinces/cities. Its imports declined by 2.4%, the steepest decline among the five coastal provinces/cities.

Guangdong, one of China's top foreign trade provinces, is experiencing a similar situation. To address this situation, the central government and the local governments have introduced a series of related policies to expedite the transformation and upgrading of the traditional processing-type enterprises. These policies include tax reductions for the enterprises to relieve their financial burden in international competition, and increasing government support for industry, learning and research to nurture new competitiveness.

For the global economy, for an extended period in the future, the main theme will be adjustment, and the coexistence of competition and cooperation will be the mainstream activity, and friction will become a normal occurrence. The global economy will slowly recover, new growth strategies are being adjusted, the global economic pattern will undergo deep changes, and the gaming between developed economies and emerging market economies will continue. The gaming between developed economies and emerging market economies, and the gaming among developing economies, will focus on the gaming between China and the US.

During the G20 London Summit in 2009, China and the US were the focus of global attention. Many people harboured their hopes for rescuing the global economy on the cooperation between China and the US. For a time, a lot of media, experts, scholars and even government officials were talking about the concept of "G2". The authors' view is that as a developing country, China is still not in a position to shoulder the responsibilities inherent in the "G2" title. Indeed, global economic issues need to be resolved by pooling together the strengths of all the countries in the world.

China is the biggest creditor for the US, and the US is one of China's biggest trade partners. The two countries have broad and deep relationships in various economic and social realms. The international financial crisis has dealt a heavy blow on China. The "world factory" mode is running into difficulties, and China's economic transition and upgrading cannot be accomplished overnight. Dubbed "world shoe capital", Dongguan has been facing hardships since 2011. The volume of orders for shoes from European and US markets is in gradual decline. Even during the peak season of Christmas in 2011, the ship loading rate for the European market was only around 50%, and that for the US market was also under 80%. Although there was a slight increase in orders from the Middle East, Latin American and African markets, this will never make up for the decline in orders from the European and US markets.

In sum, the best result of this gaming will be "inclusive growth" realised in the global context. This means carrying out adjustments and reforms on the basis of the existing global economic governance mechanism, so that the developing countries will have a greater voice. It also means enabling economic globalisation and the fruits of economic development to benefit all countries, all territories and all communities, so that they can achieve coordination in their economic and social development in the context of sustainable development. The core of "inclusive growth" is "sharing", and the aim is to create an egalitarian environment for development for more people in the world—despite the current situation of imbalanced development and interest diversification. This was the solemn pledge made by 189 countries at the United Nations—a pledge that China has never forgotten!

Conclusion and Future Prospects

"Co-opetition": Future Pattern for the World

Since the mid-1980s, "co-opetition" has been the development trend for the global economy, against the background of globalisation of the economy and rapid development of information technology. As different economies are cooperating amidst competition, they are also deepening their competition amidst cooperation. Regional and inter-regional preferential trade agreements, as well as the WTO, have become the macro platform for co-opetition. In the first decade of the 21st century, there were changes in the pattern of co-opetition in the global market economy system, with new characteristics emerging.

Industrial transfer under the conditions of globalisation has altered the pattern of global production system. The restructuring of global industries is not just the transfer of certain traditional industries, but to an even greater extent it is also the transfer of emerging industries. It is not just domestic restructure of industries, but global restructure of industries. In this restructure, developed countries are transferring labour-intensive and resource-intensive industries to developing countries and economies. This includes the labour-intensive production processes of high-tech industries. This suggests that the industrial restructure under the conditions of high technology not only involve the cross-border transfer of entire industries, but more importantly it involves the cross-border transfer of certain production processes of the same industry. In the operation of the business, the output party focuses on the key technology and controls the core business, and at the same time outsources the other processes (including the production and service processes with scientific contents and higher added value) in the form of commissioned processing, to create a new type of outsourcing processing trade. This industrial restructure, conducted through economic globalisation, creates a large volume of intra-industry trade, and forms a new world production system.

Under the conditions of economic globalisation, different economies show different levels of core competitiveness in participating the global economy—there is diversification. Mostly, the advantages of high-tech industries are the core competitiveness of developed countries. In the first decade of the 21st century, a new global economy phenomenon appeared. Some countries do not possess world-top high technology, yet they benefit from very good "late-mover advantage". They produce products on a large scale to gain cost advantage—for instance, the IT industry among the newly industrialised economies. Some ride on low costs or extensive sales networks as their core competitiveness, and sell products from other countries to the whole world. On top of this, they even grasp certain processes in the global division-of-labour industry chain and engage in specialized mass production. This also presents strong potentials for economic growth. In short, if a country can incorporate the constraints in domestic resources and exercise its comparative advantage, then it will be able to develop its core competitiveness with local characteristics in economic globalisation.

In the first decade of the 21st century, the strength of the powerful countries in the global economy is manifested in their power to control. The truly powerful countries are those that can truly control the direction of flow of global resources (petroleum, talents and capital, etc.), and also the direction of flow of global economic outputs (the sales flow of strategic products, high-tech products). They are the countries that ride on the core of product standards and a totally new set of business game rules, to control and integrate global resources for their own use. The greatest beneficiaries from globalisation are those countries that use high-tech innovation as the basis to control the flow of global resources and economic output, ultimately setting the game rules to safeguard their interest in the global economy.

In the first decade of the 21st century, international trade protection has become increasingly serious due to the unbalancedness in the economic development of various countries, the competitiveness in industry and trade, the conflicts of regional trade groups, the contradictions in the distribution of trade benefits, and the politicisation of trade issues. After this international financial crisis, trade protectionism may become more and more intensified in the global context.

The first decade of the 21st century also saw the rise of regional cooperation and deep rooted changes in the international economic pattern. The new round of WTO talks has been progressing slowly—it even ground to a halt for a period of time after the failure of the Cancun Conference in 2003. On 1 August 2004, members of the WTO reached a framework agreement after a new round of multi-lateral trade talks. However, the principles were too generalised, and there was great discrepancy among members in the area of entry into agricultural and non-agricultural markets. Then in 2006 the various countries suspended the Doha round of talks. Under these circumstances, there was development and new trends in regional trade cooperation with the Regional Trade Agreements (RTA) as the major format. In recent years, the influence of the trade talk countries formed by developing countries (such as China, India and Brazil), with the south-south cooperation as basis, has been growing. The above practices have been strategically at play as various countries vie for markets, expand their space for development, and raise their international economic status. This has had great impact on the global economic pattern.

The first decade of the 21st century also saw the growing polarization of different communities among middle income countries, low income countries, and even the poorest countries. The differences among them have appeared in terms of views on economic growth, policy direction, and foreign economic relationships.

For instance, China is the largest developing country in the world.

Due to differences in the level of development, the competition between China and the developed industrialised countries are mainly limited to the so-called "sunset industries". Although sometimes the competition is fierce, these are just hiccups in their complementary relationships. On the other hand, China's relationship with other developing countries is characterised by competition in the context of cooperation, and the trend of competition is getting more and more obvious. This is often discovered in China's relationship with other developing countries as they build economic relationships. In general, there are fewer differences between China and other members of the developing world in terms of economic structure, resource endowment, inventory of factors, demand levels, and science and technology. There is also weaker asymmetry in their complementary and mutually dependent relationships. As a result, apart from cooperation between China and other developing countries due to mutual benefit, there is also conflict and competition in the import of foreign capital and the fight for international assistance, especially in the fight for export markets. Countries and territories at different levels of economic development are already looking at and trying to solve these conflicts and contradictions, to overcome the negative impact of this new binary structure on economic development.

In short, the relationship of co-opetition will be at play in the gaming process among the participants in international economic activities, and also in the process of sustainable development in the global economy. The relationships among the competitors will also shift from the original pure confrontational competition to a certain degree of cooperation. They will be cooperating in competition, and competing in cooperation. They will be solving problems in the process of competition and cooperation, and driving developments in the same process too. The result of the game will be that the various stakeholders participating the co-opetition will benefit from the process.

"Change" and "Revolution": The Future of the China Factor

24 June 2012 is a day that all Chinese should keep in mind. On this

day, the Shenzhou 9 Spaceship took to the skies with the dream of the Chinese, and successfully performed the historic coupling with Tiangong 1 Space Station—all in the vast space. Also on this very day, Chinese Jiaolong Manned Submersible dived down to an unprecedented depth of 7,020 metres. So on this same day, the "dragon of the orient" ——China completed the dual feat of "going up to the sky and going deep into the sea" after a break of hundreds of years.

The Chinese dream is not just to pursue achievements in space and in the ocean. The Chinese also long to better understand this vast Earth, to expand their horizon on the map of global economy, to exercise their ambitious heart, to carve out their path in the adversities of the global economy, and to build a future that belongs to China. In the 21st century, China will reform and open up to even greater depths, and this will be the attitude with which China will face the world.

As a big developing country in the global economy, China will experience new development trends and directions. It will face a different international economic and political environment. This will offer a new direction for continued pursuit for the older generation, middle generation and new generation of Chinese.

China should position itself as a big responsible developing country, having a concern for domestic developments, and deepening every project of reform. The Chinese should take an integrative and balanced stance in participating in the setting of G20 issues, driving the development of the Doha talks, maintaining the benefits of China and developing countries, and upholding the principle of "a big country is the key, the environment is of first priority, developing countries are the base, and multi-lateralization is the stage". China should make reference to various international, regional and inter-regional economic cooperation organisations, and implement integrated strategies for global and regional coordination.

People often say that history will predict the future. China has implemented its reform and opening-up for over 30 years, and entered into WTO for over 10 years. The enormous achievements have impressed the world, and boosted the confidence of the people. In the World Village of the 21st century, China will be a strong, affluent and civilised member. The effort the country has made in contribution to the world is not just limited to the "four great inventions" in history. It is also evident in the contributions and promotions of today and tomorrow.

"Embrace" and "Tolerate": Future of the Global Economy

It is often said that the basis of international politics is power and authority, while the basis of international economy is benefit. Driven by benefits, various countries either cooperate in alliance, or engage in fierce and cruel competition, and the two are just one step apart. All the significant milestones in human history are invariably tied up with the changes and revolutions surrounding productivity. The four great inventions represent not only the progress of human civilisation, but also the manifestation of the prosperity of ancient China. The establishment of the global Internet transformed the Americans from "a race on car wheels" into "a race on the Internet". The knowledge-based economy of today has categorised the active participants into people who use their bodies and people who use their brains. China's ancient wisdom goes: "People who use their brains manage people; people who use their bodies are managed by others." This had found new meaning in the new pattern of global economy. The "centre-periphery" positioning for the developed countries and the developing countries in the world becomes valid once again in the revolution of science and technology.

In the revolution of the global economy, there appeared the phenomenon of "centre-periphery". The achievements of the human race in the 20th century include space exploration, information technology, life sciences, and nuclear applications. These achievements are either macro and on a very vast scale, or very micro and on a very small scale. The knowledge-based economy—in the creation of benefits and the process of distribution—formed a situation where in the "centre-periphery" structure, all the benefits of the 20th century science and technology always flow from the periphery to the centre. The result of this is that affluence accumulates on one end, and poverty accumulates on the other. When developing countries set their own economic goals, they tend (consciously or subconsciously) to look at the present state of developed country as the future state of themselves. In fact, developed countries behave on the basis of enjoyment and pleasure at the expense of extravagant consumption of resources to the detriment of nature, and this is definitely what developing countries should not emulate. Developing countries, and the entire human race for that matter, should try to grope a new and sustainable economic development goal and strategy for themselves and for the coming generations.

In the first decade of the 21st century, the human race experienced a global financial storm. Even today, the impact of this crisis is still evident—many European countries are still struggling in the pain of the debt crisis, and the dire prospect of Greece withdrawing from the Euro zone is dealing a heavy blow to the stability of the European Union.

The rescue plan to save Spain is tickling the nerves of the European Union member countries. The national credit rating for many European countries like Portugal, Spain and Italy have been dragged down. Indeed, European countries are busy dealing with their own issues. A number of Western European countries, headed by Germany, are reluctant to shoulder the debts of the Mediterranean countries, and this dragged Europe into a vicious cycle of recession. The US, on the other side of the Atlantic, is also faced with a pessimistic economic situation. The constantly expanding scope of European recession is impacting on US exports and hindering their economic recovery. The net assets of the American families have shrunk drastically, resulting in the incurring of heavy debts. The adjustment to the mode of economic development has become a common issue for emerging market economies. In the face of the threatening situation in foreign trade, the emerging market economies have numerous difficulties to deal with.

The history of global economy has shown that international economic relationships should be orderly rather than disorderly. The basis for the new international economic order is the old order, and the change and replacement of one for the other is clearly the accumulation of improvement processes—a process of quantitative change gradually becoming qualitative change. This change is definitely not driven by goodwill, but the result of a compromise between benefits and strength. It is inevitable that today's global economy and international relations are led by the developed countries. However, this situation will change with the increasing economic strength of the developing countries, and with people making new demands on social and economic life. At the same time, the "centre-periphery" structure in international economic relationships will experience corresponding changes too.

The development trend of the future global economy is a growth process of slow recovery. Adjustment will be the theme for an extended period in the future. The coexistence of competition and cooperation will be the mainstream of the future world, and trade friction will be the new norm for the global economy.

The various issues existing in the world today—environment, poverty, south-north disparity and racial issues—need to be solved and to be overcome with the shared wisdom and power of all the people in the world. The best solution to these issues is "inclusive economic growth". This means optimising the allocation of resources in the global context, narrowing the rich-poverty gap, welfare sharing and sustainable development, and fundamentally solving the double deficit of society and environment.

Here, I would like to quote from South Africa's first black president (also hailed as "National Father of South Africa") Nelson Mandela:

"I have fought against white domination, and I have fought against black domination. I have cherished the ideal of a democratic and free society in which all persons live together in harmony and with equal opportunities. It is an ideal which I hope to live for and to achieve. But if needs be, it is an ideal for which I am prepared to die."

(Nelson Mandela's statement from the dock at the opening of his trial for treason in Rivonia, April 1964)

People are born equal. No matter where they are, and what colour their skin, they should possess equal rights to enjoy what life has to offer—sunlight, dew, wealth, laughter...

References

黄卫平，刘一姣．入世十年，中国改变世界格局．社会观察，2012（1）

黄卫平，朱文晖．温特制：美国新经济与全球产业重组的微观基础．美国研究，2004（2）

黄卫平，丁凯．2010 年世界经济形势回顾与展望．当代世界，2011（1）

黄卫平．世界经济格局的变化与中国经济发展．理论视野，2011（1）

黄卫平，宋晓恒．应对气候变化挑战的全球合作框架思考——写在哥本哈根会议开幕之际．经济理论与经济管理，2010（1）

黄卫平，丁凯．对深化经济增长模式变革的再思考．学术前沿，2012（1）

黄卫平，刘一姣．2010：影响中国经济的新思考．人民论坛，2010（36）

黄卫平．世界经济格局的变化与中国经济发展．理论视野，2011（1）

黄卫平等．看不懂的世界经济．北京：经济日报出版社，2008

黄卫平．世界经济：竞合格局的变化．经济界，2007（5）

黄卫平，胡玫．美国次贷危机：对世界经济格局的再思考．美国研究，2009（2）

丁凯，黄卫平．次贷危机后的中国产业发展模式选择．江淮论坛，2012（3）

胡玫，黄卫平．升值压力下对人民币汇率问题的几点思考．国际贸易，2010（6）

裴长洪，王宏森．入世十年与中国对外贸易发展．中国经济时报，

2011 - 12 - 09

　　张燕生．全球经济失衡与中美的调整责任．当代世界，2012（2）

　　张燕生．关于全球经济失衡的探究．宏观经济管理，2011（1）

　　朱光耀．推动国际金融体系改革建立国际金融新秩序．中国财政，2010（3）